I Was There:

The Jewish Olive Grower Who Knew Jesus

by Rabbi Michael Mayersohn

Dedication

I dedicate this work of fiction to my very real students, in churches throughout Southern California and Arizona and the clergy I was able to teach in the diocese of Nottingham in central England. I frequently am reminded of the rabbinic insight which suggests, "Much have I learned from my teachers and more from my students." You have all enriched my life greatly and helped me to learn about your faith and therefore my own. Whatever distinguishes us in faith is greatly eclipsed by what draws us together and makes us one, lovers of God and students of the Almighty.

I also dedicate this work to my wife, Caryn, the woman I love, the woman who guides me and grounds me. You gently and lovingly remind me that I do not live in the 1st century and your kindness is my guiding beacon. It is a complete joy to walk this amazing journey with you, to always be able to carry your love and support wherever we go.

Rabbi Michael Mayersohn

Table of Contents

Introduction

The public events depicted here in this work
of historical fiction all happened and most of the
characters, with the notable exception of Micah and
Shoshanah and their family, lived in the times
described, what we have come to know as the first
century CE. Jesus of Nazareth, son of Joseph and
Mary, his apostles and the Roman officials all lived
during the times under consideration. Every quote
ascribed to Jesus during his adult years is taken
directly from the gospel of Matthew in the New
Testament, as is the historical narrative. I have
injected Micah and Shoshanah, a Jewish couple
living in Nazareth, their family, and a few associates
to convey how a Jewish character living at the time
of Jesus might have reacted to his life, ministry and
legacy.

I will call Jesus by his Roman name rather than his Hebrew name, Yeshua, for reasons of convention, as that is how English speakers know his name. The same is true of the apostles, whom we will call by names familiar to English speakers. At times I will use Hebrew terms with the English translation in parentheses initially and then I'll continue with the Hebrew term throughout.

My hope through this novel is to facilitate the reader's understanding of the reactions of many Jews to the ministry of Jesus. The Jews who were aware of the Jesus movement responded contemporaneously to the questions that arose from his life and death. Predictably, Jews reacted in various ways to what he had to say and what he did. Micah offers us insight into one of the paths Jews walked during and in the wake of the movement that came to be known, decades after his death, as Christianity. Jews and Christians today are the spiritual descendants of those who lived at that time, hearing the message of this Jewish teacher and responding in distinct and different ways. My hope now is that Micah, the Jew of two thousand years ago, and in the post-script, his grandson, Avi, can help us understand the events of these tumultuous times better. As we understand each other more fully we can love each other more truthfully and honestly.

Rabbi Michael Mayersohn 5777/2016

Chapter 1

News From Bethlehem

Winter brings welcome showers, even downpours to my familiar hills of the Galilee. These are the only months the rain falls and our orchards and fields depend on a good season of water from the heavens. Winter rains can soak the body until even the soul seems to shiver in hopes of finding some warmth. I know I should love the cold and rain since it is so necessary for the earth and our crops, but it comes with shorter days, less hours of sunlight, long hours of cold dark night.

My name is Micah son of Shabbetai and I live in the town of Nazareth in the region of Galilee, known to the Roman rulers as the northern region of Palestine. Rome rules all of Palestine and one of the advantages of living in a small, unimportant town is that Roman soldiers and officials never pass through. They have a camp in Tiberias, the city on the shores of the Sea of Galilee, but Nazareth, a day's hike from Tiberias, is not important enough to bring the soldiers. It is just as well because we do not need their arrogance and ruthless demonstrations of power. We in Nazareth are just as happy to be a forgotten town on the road to nowhere, a town ignored by Rome and its army.

Like my father and his father before him, I grow olives and press the olives into olive oil. We sell the oil in neighboring towns and have earned a good reputation for high quality oil. People cook with the oil, use it for lamps to bring light to the night and some even put it on their skin. Eighteen months ago, when I reached the age of eighteen, my parents arranged my marriage to Shoshanah, the daughter of a merchant family in Nazareth. I had known her since we were children, a natural situation when one lives in a small village. I agreed with the general assessment that she was the prettiest girl in town and smart too. She was learning how to sew from her mother and was starting to make beautiful tallitot (prayer shawls) that she sold at the local market. I would tie the tzitzit (the biblically commanded knotted fringes at the four corners of the shawl) when she finished and always admired the skills she had learned so well from her mother. Between the olive oil and the tallitot we had, as a young married couple, enough money to feed ourselves, help our parents and now we were able to start a family. What a joy it was when Shoshanah told me she was pregnant with our first child, the next generation of our families, the promise of a future here in Nazareth.

Times were mostly good, we had enough money from our sales to sustain ourselves, not quite enough for the pilgrimages to Jerusalem we wanted to make for the festivals, but enough to provide hope. Our only real financial burden was the tax collector, a fellow Jew hired by the Romans to collect the exorbitant taxes the Romans demanded to support their government and army here in Palestine and more to send off to Rome to keep the emperor happy. We all understood we had to pay taxes, but the collector was corrupt, taking bribes from the wealthy of our area and taking more from those of us who barely got by to make up the shortfall. We resented the high taxes and we reserved our greatest bitterness for the collector's corruption.

Our Jewish life was one of the sources of uplift and deep satisfaction. I went to the synagogue in Nazareth every Shabbat (Sabbath) to hear the reading of the week's Torah (the first books of the Bible, Genesis to Deuteronomy) portion and the reading of the Haftarah, a passage from the prophets. Mostly the Jewish men in town gathered in the synagogue to talk about the events of the day, the successes and failures of our business and what was happening among other families in town. During the week I prayed three times daily, observed the dietary restrictions of the Torah and celebrated the festivals as my people always have, with joy and devotion to tradition. Shoshanah and I put a few coins away in a jar whenever we could to save for a pilgrimage to Jerusalem for one of the three festivals. How wondrous that would be to go to the Temple, make offerings to the Lord in fulfillment of the Torah requirements. We had some friends who had done so and they described the huge crowds gathered at the Temple, the throngs of Jews coming together in the holy city to make offerings to God as our people has done for centuries. Even our first ancestor, Abraham, had made offerings here in the Land of Israel, and when commanded by God to offer his son Isaac on Mt. Moriah, he obeyed until the angel stopped him. Now Mt. Moriah, where the binding of Isaac took place, was the very site of the Temple that Solomon and then Herod the Great himself had built. We can

11

dream and hope that one day we could make that journey south, through Samaria, up the hills from the depths of the Jordan Valley and up to the crowning heights of Jerusalem. A young Jewish man can hope and dream.

My association with the Pharisees only strengthened over time. I know that when people go to Jerusalem for pilgrimage they are led by the Sadducees, who are in charge at the Temple and the Sanhedrin. I know the Sadducees work closely, maybe at times too closely, with the Romans to keep the peace and that without them the Romans might be even harsher to our people. But here in the Galilee, far from Jerusalem, we never hear from the Sadducees, they only seem to be the rich and powerful residing in Judea. Their faith seems paralyzed and stuck in the past—no belief in the traditions and teachings of the sages, no belief in the afterlife and resurrection just because they are not talked about in the scriptures. Teachings and tradition evolve over time and the Sadducees seem to be stuck in the past. The Pharisees are here in the Galilee, among the people, teaching, interpreting and leading the people here in our communities. Pharisees are great at arguing and when we get some folks traveling from town to town with new and different ideas, things you could never say in Jerusalem without getting in big trouble, all the Pharisees do is argue and try to show how wrong the speaker is. Our distance from Jerusalem and the Sadducees allow for some pretty wild teachings and ideas and some of them are a real break from tradition. The Pharisees, when they disagree, will argue with the person, try to show how misguided the ideas and the speaker are, but they never try to get rid of someone. We Jews love the arguing, the disputations, the back and forth of debate because we can learn from all of it. We believe that we learn from each other in debate and disputation, that in listening to another person's ideas and beliefs we will grow in our own faith. Those are just some of the reasons I and all my friends associate with the Pharisees and not the Sadducees.

Now, it was enough to hope and to live our simple lives here in Nazareth, selling olive oil and tallitot and offering prayers to God for the coming of the messiah. While the sacred books of the Torah and prophets said almost nothing about a messiah, our tradition had begun in recent generations to tell of our faith that God would anoint a person to bring an end to Roman oppression, an end to our subjugation, an end to our suffering. This messiah, the anointed one, will mean the end to all of our travails and how could one not pray for an end to Roman rule in our land? We hear rumors from time to time of someone claiming to be the anointed one, some have even raised up an army to wage war against Rome. It seems a fool's errand, since all Pontius Pilate in Jerusalem does is use his formidable army to assassinate the messianic claimant, massacre his followers or kill the leader and the people. Still, we hope that this will be the year the messiah will come and if not this year, then the next and so on. In our daily prayers and every year at the Passover dinner we express our longing for the coming of the messiah. Our faith in the promised future of redemption and liberation never ends.

This day dawned as cold as any in the Galilee and I was in Cana selling my olive oil in the marketplace. Sales were good, the day was finally getting warmer and I was looking forward to seeing Shoshanah when I went home. My cousin, Chayim, a few years older than I and son of my father's brother, is one of those people who seems to know everything, all the news of every family in the entire region. He had a certain charm, which drew people to him and made them comfortable telling him the news of the day from traveling merchants.

This day he rushed up to me panting and smiling from ear to hear, "Did you hear about Mary and Joseph from your hometown?" I had to admit I had heard the rumors, that Mary and Joseph were engaged to be married, how she had mysteriously disappeared from town and everyone thought they had anticipated the wedding day by spending the night together. People were sure she had gotten pregnant and that she was ashamed and did not want to feel the disgrace of the community, and so left to stay with relatives until the baby was born. We had all heard that Joseph, known for his quiet dignity and steady presence, went to be with her and he was being awfully quiet about the situation before he left.

Chayim practically shouted, "That's not the whole story! Mary and Joseph went to Bethlehem and had the baby there. Everyone is talking about some big mystery with the pregnancy and the speculation is all over the place. Some people even think she got pregnant by someone other than Joseph!" I had to admit that Chayim had some pretty shocking news this time and it was intriguing. What was the big mystery about this pregnancy and why go to Bethlehem of all places? We all knew Bethlehem as a quiet town south of Jerusalem that was most famous for its bakeries and the fact that a thousand years ago it was the hometown of King David, the greatest king of Israel ever. Chayim, who was pretty good at his scripture studies, reminded me of the verse from the prophet Micah, my own namesake, "But you, Bethlehem, in the land of Judah, are by no means least among the rulers of Judah; for out of you will come a ruler who will be the shepherd of my people Israel." (Micah 5:2)

"Micah, what if the prophet was talking about a messiah being born in Bethlehem? What if that's what he was talking about hundreds of years ago?" As usual, cousin Chayim kept talking, hardly taking a moment to breathe, "It's even stranger than all that. The story is that some Magi went to

Jerusalem and told Herod that Joseph and Mary's baby was the messiah, king of Israel! There are even tales about a mysterious star in the sky over Bethlehem when the baby was born. Can you imagine the messiah, born in Bethlehem like the prophet Micah said, but really coming from Nazareth of all places? And Joseph and Mary are his parents? This is huge. These are great days." Chayim finally took a breath.

I had to slow him down, "Let's think about this for a moment. Our sacred texts and the teaching of our sages is that God will anoint a person, not that the messiah will be a newborn baby. This would go against everything we have studied and learned."

"I know," Chayim interrupted, "but imagine if the messiah really has come and from your own hometown of Nazareth, born in Bethlehem like the prophet Micah, after whom you were named, might have been saying?" I had to admit the idea was awfully appealing but I still could not get over the idea of the messiah finally arriving and all these wild stories about a mysterious pregnancy. Mary and Joseph were just an ordinary Jewish couple, maybe a little more pious than most, but just regular people like the rest of us. I could not quite make sense of all this.

This was all a lot to digest and even harder to understand when I considered all the teachings of my sages. I talked to Shoshanah about it and she seemed to think it was all possible and just hoped it was all true. "Micah, I know what cousin Chayim is saying is exciting and overwhelming, but what are the chances the messiah is born from a family in Nazareth of all places?"

"I know, Shoshanah, there are so many reasons not to believe Joseph and Mary's baby is the messiah, but what if he is? What if this is what we have been waiting for all these years? It would change everything."

The rest of my family was divided, some wanting to believe, the others reminding me that none of our sages had ever mentioned the messiah being born as a baby. The whole idea was that God would anoint a person, an adult, to be the messiah and that that person would lead our people to the end of history, the end of Rome, the end of all suffering. We argued, debated and studied and wondered if the time had finally come or if this was just one more empty story ending with no messiah and more disappointment for all of us. We Jews love to worry and this seemed like just one more reason to fret.

Months later we were, as usual, focused back on making a living, not worrying much about what was happening in Jerusalem or Bethlehem or anywhere else, just selling jars of olive oil, creating tallitot for people to wear on Shabbat and studying the scriptures. Herod had died but nothing else changed. One of his sons, Herod Antipas now was ruler only in the Galilee since none of his sons was strong enough to rule over all Palestine as "the Great" was. Antipas followed in the tyrannical footsteps of his father and we just had to avoid running into any Roman government officials. That mostly meant avoiding Tiberias, the regional capital, built up by Antipas as his seat of power.

Months after the death of Herod we received great news. Joseph and Mary and their baby were coming home to Nazareth. We had heard they had fled to Egypt to avoid the wrath of Herod. He had apparently heard some of the rumors, that some baby born in Bethlehem to a couple from Nazareth was being proclaimed by some to be the long-awaited Jewish messiah. He knew enough of Jewish teachings about the messiah that anyone, even a baby, who was being talked about as a messiah could be a threat to him and Rome. Now that Herod was dead they were on their way back to Nazareth. When they arrived we all clamored to see them, to see the baby and to ask, as carefully as we could, about the stories we had heard. The baby, whom they called Jesus, looked pretty ordinary, like any other baby we had ever seen. He certainly did not look like any messiah or king of Israel, just a baby. Joseph and Mary were pretty circumspect about the circumstances of his birth, just saying that the baby was a gift from God. Lots of parents felt that way, but they seemed to be keeping a secret and none of us could figure it out. Mary nursed the baby and told the other women in town how blessed they felt, but nothing about him being the messiah or anything beyond what all parents said about their children.

With Mary, Joseph and Jesus back in Nazareth, things quieted down, no one was talking any more about this baby being the messiah and if anyone did start speculating at the synagogue, they quieted down as soon as the family came in. Nazareth was just an ordinary town that no one took note of, the baby Jesus was just another Jewish baby, nothing special, and all that conversation and guessing and pondering just died out. In just a few years, Shoshanah's and my baby, Rachel, was growing up, and she was just months younger than Jesus and they had become friends. Jesus was just another little boy in Nazareth.

Chapter 2

This Boy, Jesus

By the time he was seven years old, no one was talking about Jesus being any different from any other young Jewish boy in Nazareth. Rachel played with him when the boys allowed, and when I asked her about him she looked at me quizzically. "Abba (father), why do you ask about him and none of the other children in town? What do you think makes him different from any of the other children I know?"

"I was just wondering," I asked, "if he seemed more pious, special, in any way different from other children in town."

"Abba, you are being weird and other than the fact that he does not have any brothers or sisters, he is no different from the other children. You embarrass me when we are in the marketplace and you watch him more closely than anyone else."

I had to admit that he had caught my eye but I could not explain to my oldest child what I had heard about him from his birth. None of the adults in town talked about it anymore, probably to respect the privacy of his parents, Joseph and Mary.

I had to admit that when he came over to play with Rachel and our two younger sons, when they all ran and played, he seemed just like all the other children. He even got in trouble once or twice, although usually he was well behaved and would wander off into the fields by himself. That did seem strange, I would see him from time to time just wander off by himself into the fields and he appeared to be, well, pensive and introspective. Once I summoned up the nerve to ask him about his solo walks among the hills around town and he explained, "I like to be by myself and think and sometimes I pray when I'm alone."

"You are seven years old and you go off by yourself to pray?" I asked, hoping I did not seem too intrusive or probing of a young child.

He did not seem to mind or take offense. "I think about the world and how people treat each other and wish things were different, that people would consider not only how they behaved, but also how they felt, the emotions they harbor. I think people would act differently if they could bring themselves to feel differently. And I pray to God that He will be with me during my life."

I had to admit that my daughter was both right and wrong. This boy, Jesus, was just like all the other children, he liked to run and play, but he was also completely different from any other child I had known. How could I resolve this discrepancy, how a child could be just like other children and profoundly different at the same time? And why would a young child be praying to God on his own without his teachers and sages instructing him on the prayers of our people? It was all so perplexing.

About two years later, when Jesus and my daughter, Rachel, were both nine years old I took note of Jesus in the synagogue. While the other children whispered among themselves and begged their parents to be able to play outside, Jesus sat with the adults. He didn't just sit with the adults, he seemed purposely to sit near the elders and sages of the synagogue, the people all the other children avoided. When they sat and talked about the teachings of the Torah and argued among themselves the boy, Jesus, sat with them and listened with rapt attention. It was clear he was absorbing everything they were saying, learning from them and he even argued with them from time to time. They smiled warmly even when he offered insights they found objectionable because it was so unusual for a child to be interested in scriptures and the teachings of the sages. Jesus' father, Joseph,

27

would sit a few feet away, watching his son, admiring the boy's intelligence, curiosity and insights and wondering where it all came from. I knew Joseph fairly well since Nazareth was a small town and when I pointed out to him how unusual the boy, Jesus, was, he smiled with pride. He even reminded me of the stories his father, Jacob, and grandfather, Matan, used to tell about the family tree reaching back over twenty generations from Jesus back to King David. We got a good laugh out of the irony—here was this precocious, insightful child, Jesus, and the family tradition that he was a descendant of King David himself. Maybe it was true after all.

One year after we had a special luncheon on the occasion of my daughter turning twelve years old, it was time to celebrate the bar mitzvah of her friend, our family friend, Jesus. He was at our house so often, playing with Rachel and the younger boys that sometimes it felt like he was part of the family.

He did not have his own siblings, so it seemed like he took on our three children as his own brothers and sister. Now it was time for his bar mitzvah and we were definitely part of the celebration. Other boys read from the week's Torah portion, recited the blessings and offered a few insights about the Torah portion to show they had learned from their teachers. We knew to expect something different, something special from Jesus and we were not disappointed. The Shabbat morning of his becoming bar mitzvah was a day of anticipation in the community. We had all come to expect something special from Jesus and we soon saw what it was. We offered the Shabbat morning prayers, and arrived pretty quickly at the time of the reading of the Torah portion from the book of Exodus. Jesus recited the prayers flawlessly and then read the Torah portion beautifully, reminding us all of the greatest teachers of our small town. This thirteen year old boy sounded like the teachers who had been reading Torah their entire lives. We looked at each other knowingly, remembering all those times Jesus sat with the elders and sages while the children played outside.

He offered his insights into the experience of becoming a bar mitzvah:

Our people, led by Moshe Rabbeinu (Moses, our teacher) fled slavery in Egypt to be free so they could worship and serve God. Today we are still drawn to worship and serve God with all our heart, soul and might. Sometimes I see our Jewish people devoted to doing what God wants them to do as our sages have taught us over the generations. I think we can go further than that, beyond just obeying God with our actions and serve God with our love, heart and spirit. What if we, in addition to keeping kosher, observing Shabbat and the festivals, supporting the offerings at the Temple in Jerusalem, what if we went beyond all that and served God with love and our spirit, not just with our hands and bodies? What if we did not just observe the commandments to not murder, for

instance, but committed ourselves to not being

angry with our neighbors either? What if we

committed to not just love our neighbor but even

loved our enemy?

Wouldn't that be serving God with not just

our actions, but with our heart and soul too? What

kind of community could we create if we really

devoted ourselves to God with every part of our

being?

And then he stopped, just like that. People
were stunned and looked at each other in disbelief.
They asked each other, "What did we just hear?"
They were stunned with his maturity, his insights
and his devotion to God. All the adults of the
synagogue gathered around him after his words
and greeted him with words of welcome. Now with
his bar mitzvah celebration he could participate
fully in the life of the synagogue and there would be
less amazement when he sat with the elders and

sages. He was truly something special and we all knew it, even at the young age of thirteen. We looked at each other and wondered what would come of this special boy.

My family and Joseph, Mary and Jesus had become close over the years and we had started to celebrate Passover together in one home or the other. Joseph and I would slaughter two of our chickens, pluck their feathers and drain the blood. Mary and Shoshanah went to the marketplace to buy horseradish and wine. Their favorite stop was going to the baker, who had cleaned out all his equipment and made the matza (unleavened bread), the large round and wavy sheets that were so central to the celebration. While doing all the preparations we all dreamt of how it would be when one day we could make the Passover pilgrimage to Jerusalem and be part of the festivities and crowds there. Joseph and I imagined what it would be like to be in the Temple and having bought a lamb with our saved money, seeing the Levites in the Temple make the requisite sacrifice. That night of our Passover celebration in Jerusalem we would eat the lamb of our sacrificial offering, surrounded by our children and we knew it would be a great festival night. It was a sweet fantasy and we could not know if we would ever be able to do it in reality.

During the Passover dinner that night, there in Nazareth, Jerusalem still a far-off dream, we all ate the Passover foods, recited the passages from Exodus and retold the story of our Israelite ancestor slaves fleeing Egypt. We even let the older children drink the required four cups of wine, each cup representing one of God's promises to redeem the Israelites from slavery. There was one strange and mystifying moment and I am not sure even Mary and Joseph noticed. At one point, with everyone talking and eating and laughing I noticed Jesus, sitting quietly, holding a piece of matza and the cup of wine, seeming lost in the moment. He looked at the symbolic foods, the matza representing the bread of affliction, the wine, a symbol of our joyous redemption and he just gazed at them. He held both in his hands for several moments and seemed lost in thought. I knew better than to ask what he was thinking about because when I had done so before, Jesus would just say he was thinking and praying. We ended the Passover meal with the familiar prayerful words and hope, "L'shanah haba'ah B'Yerushalayim," "Next Year in Jerusalem."

I had the good fortune to watch Jesus grow from childhood to the young man he became. So many of us admired him and found him to be something of a rebel and a man of personal and religious integrity. He clearly cared deeply about God and Judaism and he approached the world and all living things with love and respect. Knowing him from his earliest days to now as a young adult, I had the overwhelming sense that great things would come of and from him and that he would have a considerable impact on our community and beyond. What I could never imagine is just how curious, impactful and interesting his life would be and how many would be touched by it for years to come.

Chapter 3

A Most Curious Ministry Begins

As a family friend of Joseph, Mary and Jesus, the young man's trip out of Nazareth seemed to come out of nowhere and to have been totally predictable all at the same time. I asked Joseph about it and he answered somewhat cryptically that the young man left on a journey south he had to take. I had the sense there was something Joseph was not telling me, and I knew his family needed their privacy. We all had the sense that something momentous was going to happen in Jesus' life.

After a few weeks, he returned to Nazareth and although he did not stay long, he had an amazing tale to tell all of us at the synagogue. He told us of his journey south and how he heard stories about a man named John who was gathering crowds to a remote desert spot in Judea. Our own Sea of Galilee, just a day's hike from Nazareth, empties into the Jordan River and the river courses south and then it flows into the Sea of Salt, or as many now were calling it, the Dead Sea. Both names were apt as it was the saltiest body of water we knew about and nothing could live in it due to the salt. Right there where the Jordan River flows into the Sea of Salt this man, John, was drawing crowds.

What we learned about this man whom people were starting to call John the Baptist is that he was doing something a bit odd. People would come down from Jerusalem, about twenty miles away, and this John would immerse them in the waters of the Jordan River. He declared to people, "Repent, for the kingdom of heaven is near." Throngs of people came to him with hope in their hearts that if people would repent, God's kingdom and the end of Roman oppression would be close. Some even suggested that this John was the one whom the prophet Isaiah was talking about when he declared, "A voice of one calling in the desert, 'Prepare the way for the Lord, make straight paths for him.'" They pointed out that John wore clothes made of camel's hair and he wore a leather belt and ate locusts! The murmur was how this was so reminiscent of what we knew about the prophet Elijah, who wore the same exact clothing. Our people had been teaching for generations that Elijah would announce the coming of the messiah.

Jesus told us the story of his meeting with John the Baptist when John was immersing people in the water. Jesus apparently asked John to baptize him as he had done for hundreds of other pilgrims and John rather cryptically and with great confidence said to Jesus, "I need to be baptized by you, and you come to me?" Jesus told us he insisted that John baptize him and when John did, everything went still and a bat kol (voice from heaven), could be heard saying, "This is my son, whom I love, with him I am pleased."

The adults all looked at each other. What were we to make of this moment Jesus was describing? We were familiar with what the sages described as the bat kol, a voice from heaven, God's voice coming down to correct, instruct, or inform us of God's wishes. We are all sons or children of God, so what did it mean when God said to Jesus that he was God's son? We also speculated about this John baptizing people and ultimately baptizing Jesus. Everyone was, of course, familiar with the teaching from the Torah (Numbers 19) that the waters of purification could cleanse people, especially priests, of their impurity. Every Jew knew about the sources of impurity, from contact with the dead, menstrual bleeding and other normal life activities. The waters of purification did not cleanse people of physical uncleanliness but the state of impurity that all people experienced from time to time. This John was baptizing people, a ritual he considered an act of repentance for sin. The sages had never addressed the question of water as an element of repentance for sin. John had added a new twist to the teaching on the spiritual cleansing nature of water in Judaism. John the Baptist was immersing people in water as an act of repentance for sin and Jesus apparently sought that ritual that became known as baptism. These are fascinating times in which we are living when people can take old traditions and reframe them for new ideas, new purposes. We have to wonder if this will catch on and become bigger than John baptizing people in the Jordan River.

As Jesus told us about this powerful experience he had with John the Baptist down at the Jordan River near the Sea of Salt we all came to believe that something important was happening. This John fellow was taking old rituals and changing them into something we had not known before and Jesus was starting to teach ideas with which we were not familiar. None of the adults in Nazareth were quite sure what to make of all this, but many of us, myself included, were intrigued and drawn to these new ideas. That was one of the great things about the Galilee, we were far enough away from Jerusalem and the Sadducees that we could learn about new rituals, new teachings and no Sadducees were around to stop us. The Pharisees might argue their authenticity, but no one could or would stop what was happening.

Just like that, with no warning, we learned that Jesus, now a young man in his twenties, moved down from the hills of Nazareth, to the town of Capernaum (K'far Nachum, the village of Nachum in Hebrew) on the shores of the Sea of Galilee. This was a thriving village with an active fishing industry and many more people than in Nazareth. It seems Jesus was drawn to a larger community, a place with more people and more activity than one could find in Nazareth. I talked to Shoshanah about it and we decided that what was happening with our family friend, Jesus, was getting too big to ignore or overlook and potentially too important to watch from a distance. We talked to his parents, Joseph and Mary, and they felt that as his parents they had to stay home and not interfere with what their son was doing. Shoshanah and I decided that I would go to Capernaum to join Jesus and his growing band of followers, even though I was considerably older than they were. I had to see for myself what was going on.

Chapter 4

The Teacher Teaches, a Leader Leads

With the move to Capernaum, even though temporary for me, I had to acknowledge that I considered myself a follower of this young man, Jesus. I was no longer simply watching him grow up, watching him at the Passover table, observing him at the synagogue as he both delighted and disturbed the synagogue leaders with his wisdom and insights. Now I knew him to be something special, a man with godly gifts as a teacher and leader. Something was going on in his life that we all had to acknowledge and even his critics knew he had to be taken seriously.

I continued to be amazed at the strong attachment people were making to Jesus. As people heard about him or heard from him, large numbers were drawn to his character and his message. Then there were the very few who came close to him, not the big crowds, but the few who became part of his inner circle, those most closely attached to him and what he was doing and teaching. In Capernaum two brothers, Simon Peter and Andrew, local fishermen, heard what Jesus had to say and quickly became part of what was becoming an intense and devoted inner circle of followers. Two more brothers, James and John, sons of a man named Zebedee, all also fishermen, attached themselves to Jesus and all of them left their work and started spending all their time with Jesus. Simon Peter, whom many called just Peter, Andrew, James and John travelled with Jesus, ate and resided with him and people came to know them as his closest followers. They taught him about fishing since he knew nothing about it, and he taught them his ideas about God and God's love for every person, even simple fishermen.

Jesus and his small coterie of devoted former fishermen, now followers and students, travelled from town to town in the Galilee and Jesus drew crowds to him wherever he went. Jews in the towns of Galilee were attracted to his message, his emphasis not so much on strict adherence to the laws as the Pharisees promoted, but to a spiritual embrace of the devotion to God beyond the laws. He never told people to stop following the laws because that was simply unimaginable, but he did want them to think about the emotions and personal needs behind the laws. No one had heard this message before because the Pharisees and sages had always focused primarily and at times solely to doing what God commanded without regard to the emotions behind the law. They even told people to follow the laws even when we did not understand them or their meaning. Many found it compelling and the crowds drawn to him grew greater by the day.

Then we started witnessing and hearing about Jesus healing people and cleansing them of evil spirits. We all knew that people got sick as a punishment for some sin they had committed and that people were troubled by evil spirits for the same reasons. Committing sins led directly to God's punishment and the only way to heal was to repent for the sins in the hopes of being forgiven. We had all heard tales of healers who could, because of their intimate relationships with God, bring forgiveness and healing to people. None of us had witnessed it in person before. As someone close to Jesus I was now able to see for myself how so many sick and troubled people came to him, repented of their sins and he offered them forgiveness. They were healed! As the word spread about Jesus being able to heal people, the sick and the lame came from all over the region, as far away as Jerusalem itself to come to him for an end to their suffering.

There were the critics, especially the leaders of the Pharisees who saw Jesus as a rebel and a critic, a person who did not teach what they had always taught. They questioned how he could claim the authority to forgive people's sins. He had not attended their academies and did not follow their established rules and now he was claiming to have the authority to forgive sins and heal. Many of the Pharisees were angry and disturbed by what they saw going on, especially the crowds that began following him wherever he went. Some of the older Pharisees were intensely jealous about the crowds yearning to be near this young man with the growing reputation for teaching, healing and cleansing.

One beautiful sunny day the crowds gathering near him to hear his words and be healed by his forgiveness grew larger than ever. His closest apostles, Peter, Andrew, James and John, as always, were closest to him. I was not quite in that inner circle, but I was an old family friend and had become a follower so I was able to hear his words first hand and witness what he was doing for myself. This day on the shores of the Sea of Galilee was different, we could all tell there was something happening spontaneously. The crowds were bigger than ever and Jesus seemed like he was ready to speak to people in a way he never had before. What we could not know that day was that this was going to be his greatest teaching message ever, a teaching that all of us would remember for years. He never spoke to anyone about being nervous before speaking to crowds of people and this time he was not nervous but there was a look of purpose and resolve in his eyes.

He began with a simple but ironic teaching that we had heard in bits and pieces before but now he had apparently organized in his own mind into a major address. His opening words were, "Blessed are the poor in spirit, for theirs is the kingdom of heaven." We looked at each other with a mixture of wonder and curiosity. What did he mean by the poor in spirit? Was he talking about people who led lives bereft of spiritual riches, people who did not lead lives of spiritual richness? He said that "theirs is the kingdom of heaven," and as followers of the Pharisees we believed in the after-life, but is that what he meant? He went on to talk about mourners, the meek and people who hunger and thirst for righteousness and in each case he suggested rewards for those we did not always associate with rewards. In our world the strong, the mighty, the rich experienced the bounties of life, not the poor or the weak or the hungry. Jesus was telling us that the world need not operate as we always believed it did, that God's blessings were available even to those whom we thought were the outcasts, those some imagined were outside God's love.

During what we came to know as a sermon right there on the hills at the shore of the Sea of

Galilee Jesus made a startling declaration that was clearly meant as a response to the elders and the Pharisees, "Do not think that I have come to abolish the Torah or the Prophets. I have come not to abolish them but to fulfill them." There had been some rumblings from the leaders of the Pharisees that his teaching was not only challenging their authority as teachers and leaders, but that his messages were contrary to the words of the Torah and the Prophets. No one in our community would tolerate someone violating the Torah and Jesus was making it clear to us that this was not his intent. We all breathed a sigh of relief when we heard this part of his sermon.

We were all riveted now to his message and hundreds, maybe thousands of people were silent in hopes of hearing his profound teaching. Citing passages from the Torah, specifically from the book of Deuteronomy, Jesus launched into a part of his sermon that addressed laws of murder, adultery, divorce, oaths, retribution and regard for enemies. In each of six cases he cited the relevant law of the Torah and then told us he wanted us to go beyond the Torah teachings. Throngs of Jews listening to Jesus' sermon heard that we should not only refrain from murdering people, but not even be angry with other people. We should not only not commit adultery, but refrain from having lust for women and that we should only get divorced if our wife is unfaithful. He concluded this part of his message by saying that we should love our enemies! Love the Romans? Love the local people who steal from us, injure us and worship idols? Jesus called us to love not just our neighbors but those whom we rightly considered enemies. Jesus was demanding, with all these calls for righteous behavior that went beyond the laws as we knew them, he was demanding that we change, fundamentally and profoundly, how we lived our lives. There was a murmur in the crowd as people debated all this and wondered if it was realistic and even possible.

We did what Jews do, no matter how compelling the teacher or sage. We argued and debated what we were hearing. There were some, predictably, who thought everything Jesus was saying was right and powerful and important for everyone to hear. Some even insisted Jesus was starting a new movement within the Pharisees with new ways of thinking about our lives and faith as Jews. And inevitably there were those who listened to Jesus who thought his ideas were just out of bounds and too far away from how we have always acted and believed as Jews. I found myself much more closely aligned with those who were attracted to what Jesus was teaching and preaching. I believed there was room to reform Jewish beliefs and practices, to change how and even why we were living the Jewish lives we were living. Jesus never suggested, for instance, that we stop keeping kosher or observing Shabbat, but that we think about how and why we were following these commandments from God. He wanted us to think about the actions we could and could not do on Shabbat and ask ourselves whether all of it made sense. Regarding the dietary laws he was asking us to think not only about what went into our mouths but what came out of them too. We had never really thought of it that way before.

His sermon continued, hundreds and hundreds of people listening, and I have to admit I cannot recall everything he said, there was so much. It was good that there were some scribes there, men who were trained to record what people said and who wrote furiously fast. Most of us could read and write but they were really good at it. In any case, some parts of the sermon I cannot recall, but there was a moment when he started talking about prayer. He told us that some people pray hypocritically, making sure people see them pray, making something of a performance or show of their piety and prayer. It was true that Jewish law said that we were supposed to pray with a minyan, a minimum of ten men, but there was also a place, Jesus was insisting, for private prayer in our Jewish lives. It was also probably true that many people paid less attention to their private prayer than their public prayer so people could see them praying and know they were praying. Lots of us wanted people to think of us as pious and devout and public prayer allowed for that perception. Here was Jesus, clearly not telling us to ignore public prayer, to stop praying in the synagogue, but his message was to focus more of our spiritual energy on private prayer. He reminded us that we cannot see God and that we did not have to be seen while we were praying to God. As was so often the case, his insights and teachings were important and profound.

Then he got really bold, doing something none of us ever expected. He told us how we should pray when we were alone. Since he composed the prayer many of us who liked it started calling it,

"Jesus' Prayer," but I think he meant it to be our prayer, not his. He was never self-centered like that to want something named after him. He offered these words for our private prayer:

Avinu Shebashamayim (Aramaic for Our Father Who is in Heaven), hallowed be your name, your kingdom come, your will be done, on earth as it is in Heaven. Give us this day our daily bread. Forgive us our debts as we also have forgiven our debtors. And lead us not into temptation, but deliver us from the evil one. For if you forgive men when they sin against you, your Heavenly Father will also forgive you. But if you do not forgive men their sins, your Father will not forgive your sins.

Who could imagine such a prayer, succinct and powerful with a clear message about forgiveness and a dynamic relationship between us and God. Jesus' prayer was telling us that God's forgiveness of us is part of our relationship with Him, that our forgiveness of the people in our lives prompts God's forgiveness of us. Conversely, the prayer suggests, if we are in a spiritual state in which we will not or cannot forgive, God withholds His forgiveness. We are praying for a world in which God's will be done here as it is in *shamayim*, the heavens. How remarkable will that be for God's will to be done here on earth, making our world a place of justice and love and mercy?

Then there is the part of the prayer that many of us struggled with—the statement that God would forgive our debts, apparently contingent on the idea that we would forgive those who owe us debts. Some people who heard the sermon were sure he had said "sins," not debts, urging us to forgive people's sins against us as God forgives our sins. Even the scribes were not all of one mind on what he actually said, sins or debts, and in either case the prayer was asking a lot of us. Were we supposed to pray that we could forgive people's debts to us and leave ourselves even poorer than we already were because debts were not being repaid? Or were we supposed to forgive the sins other people had committed against us, leaving us without our righteous grudges we had built up against those who had sinned against us? I knew that I did not want to forgive those sins, but I also wanted God to forgive my sins and how could I, Jesus seemed to be suggesting in his prayer, expect God to forgive me if I could not forgive others. This was a hard prayer to say and I have a feeling Jesus meant it to be hard. It seemed so complicated and simple at the same time, the language of the prayer was so rhythmic and lovely and Jesus was challenging us to do hard things with simple, easy language. I guess this is what prayer is supposed to be, at least what Jesus wanted prayer to be.

His sermon went on to call us to difficult goals, like not being judgmental. When I heard that I remembered all the times I had judged Shimon a couple fields over from mine when I saw him resting while I was working and I was sure he was not working hard enough. Jesus wanted us to "do to others what you would have them do to you," and reminded us that this was straight from the Torah and Prophets. Many of us, when we heard these words, were reminded of the teaching of the Torah in so many places, that we knew the heart of the stranger because we were strangers in the Land of Egypt. We remembered the words of the Torah that we were obligated to take care of the poor, those from other places who were living among us and the orphan, meaning all the weak and vulnerable among us. We knew that Jesus was building on the teaching of the Torah and calling us to fulfill all those teachings and more. His was truly a sermon of a sage, building on the teachings of the Torah and Prophets, taking his teaching to new places we had not considered before. For so many he had become our teacher and leader.

In the days after the great sermon by the shores of the sea, more and more people who were sick and possessed by demons came to Jesus for healing and he turned no one away. As some of us watched him it became clear he was exhausted and drained from all the interactions with people. We were reminded of his humanity, how even the great teacher could be worn out and just plain tired. Surrounded almost constantly by demanding crowds he could not turn away, he sailed on the sea to the distant shores and said to no one in particular, "Foxes have holes and birds of the air have nests, but the ben adam, the son of man has no place to lay his head." All of us devoted to his teaching and preaching knew that he was just tired.

One thing we had learned about our teacher Jesus was that when he became exhausted he turned to the sea to get away from the crowds. On one of these voyages on the Sea of Galilee a sudden storm picked up on the sea, waves crashing against the boat, wind pushing the sails in different direction, we all looked at each other in panic. None of us could remember a storm so fierce out here on the water before and we were afraid we were going to drown. Some of the apostles went to Jesus in hopes he could help as he did for sick people and he was, understandably, sleeping. Some of the disciples asked him to save us all from drowning and he chastised us, "You of little faith, why are you so afraid?" There was always this lesson with him that our fear was a sign of our lack of faith. He turned to the storm itself, facing the rain, the wind and the waves with fierce resolve and he seemed to rebuke all of it and the storm suddenly subsided, the rain ceased, the winds died down, the waves shrunk. I turned to a couple of his closest apostles and asked, "Exactly who do we think this Jesus is? His teachings are remarkable and unprecedented, he heals the sick and those possessed by demons and now the very forces of nature, the wind and rain obey his words? What," I asked them for the first and certainly not the last time, "is going on here, who is he?" We all looked at each other, knowing we were all asking the same questions and wondering what we were witnessing. No one had an answer, only questions.

In some surprising and odd way, the healings of sick people by Jesus were becoming routine. We saw him heal a paralytic here, a blind and mute person there. In each and every case it was clear the person had sinned and Jesus believed himself to have the authority to forgive their sins. He really wanted people to cleanse their hearts, to stop sinning, not only in their actions but in their heart and spirit too. If they had faith in Jesus, believing that he had the authority to forgive their sins and if they were sincere, he would bring them healing.

One of the challenges the Pharisees made against Jesus, beyond the obvious that they did not believe he had the authority to forgive people's sins, was his inclination to associate with all kinds of people. No one in our community liked tax collectors and we all shunned them because of their corruption and their brutal ways. But not Jesus! Our teacher sat willingly with tax collectors and other sinners, even breaking bread with them, sharing with them his ideas and lessons. When the Pharisees challenged him on this he was emphatic and firm, "It is not the healthy who need a doctor, but the sick." Jesus insisted to the Pharisees that his ministry was to people who were sinning, people who needed him and that he was not going to shun the very people he was there to heal and forgive. One of the great things about Jesus that I noticed when we traveled about was his certainty and clarity—he knew exactly what he believed and that what he was doing was right, just and loving. His confidence, his compassion and his commitment to what he was doing were inspiring.

Jesus knew he could not do all this alone. Over time he gathered around him twelve intimate apostles, those closest to him, the inner circle that had started with Peter, Andrew, James and John. Now there were twelve young men closest to him of all his apostles and he knew it was time to send them out to spread his word. He could no longer do it alone and he believed the message of his love, his spirit and compassion had to be shared with everyone. He wanted large numbers of people to recognize that what he called, "The kingdom of heaven," was imminent. His twelve apostles now had the authority to heal the sick, raise the dead and forgive people's sins. He made sure they could not be accused of profiting from their ministry and he also assured them they would face criticism and opposition from the established leaders of the community. People with power and position, he taught them, would always challenge those who came with new and different ideas. They could not be swayed or discouraged by the criticism of those who were entrenched in power. Jesus told them that their ministry, like his, was not to keep people comfortable with the way things have been but to know that everything was about to change. Parents, older people, people seduced by their own power, would all oppose them and his teachings. He needed them to know that what mattered most was his message, the approaching kingdom of heaven and God's presence in their lives.

I was too old, maybe too set in my own ways to be counted among the closest apostles, but I watched what Jesus and his apostles were doing. I frequently traveled home to Nazareth, to Shoshanah and the children and I told them one story after another. Perhaps because she was not with Jesus as much as I was, Shoshanah tended to be a bit more skeptical, reminding me that the Pharisees and their teachings had been around a long time and maybe Jesus and his apostles should not be so quick to abandon those familiar ways. "I love and admire our friend, Jesus, too, but how do we know it is true when he says this 'kingdom of heaven' is so close," she asked. "We have had our hopes built up high before only to be disappointed and downcast, so it is hard to believe," Shoshanah said to me in the quiet of the night. I knew and understood her hesitation, it had been mine as well in my most private moments, and I assured her that I kept my wits about me when I listened to him. It was just that his life and his teachings were so compelling that I had to keep close to hear and see what he was saying and doing.

Shabbat observance frequently became an issue for all of us in the Jewish community and certainly for those listening to and following Jesus. We all had to approach the local sages with questions about whether what we were doing or thinking about doing on Shabbat was permitted. Sometimes it just all seemed so complicated, so many rules and restrictions on what we could or could not do. Jesus managed to cut through all that and in his typical fashion he raised the issue to a higher level and forced us to confront our Shabbat observance questions in new ways. One Shabbat afternoon Jesus and his apostles hiked through some of the local fields of grain and a few of them spontaneously and out of their own hunger, picked some of the heads of grain to eat. Pharisee critics were always on the look-out to catch Jesus doing something forbidden and they jumped on the violation as soon as it was reported to them. We all knew from the Torah that Jews were not allowed to gather grain on Shabbat, "Six days you shall labor, but on the seventh day you shall rest; even during the plowing season and harvest you must rest." (Exodus 34:21) We had all understood that to mean that gathering grain on Shabbat was forbidden by God, that we had to gather enough on the other six days to suffice all our needs. Jesus could have argued with the Pharisees that according to another teaching in the Torah, people are permitted to take grapes or grain for yourself, presumably because you are hungry. (Deuteronomy 23:24, 25) Many of us thought that could be a good argument for Jesus to make, that his apostles were hungry and they had to eat even if it meant taking a few heads of grain on Shabbat. That was not Jesus' response, though. He firmly and confidently reminded the Pharisees that King David himself had allowed his soldiers, when they were hungry, to eat the consecrated bread of the local priest. (I Samuel 21) In his usual fashion, he was not saying the laws of the Shabbat were no longer binding or that he was here to void them, but that they had to be understood with compassion rather than the usual strictness and devotion to laws of the Pharisees. He ended that conversation pretty quickly when he mentioned David and the consecrated bread.

Shabbat observance came up again at one of the local synagogues when a person with a deformed hand was present among the congregation. Some local Pharisees taunted Jesus, asking him if he was going to violate Shabbat by healing the man's hand. Jesus rebuked them by pointing out that if one of their animals fell into a pit on Shabbat they would rescue the animal. They looked at each other and started arguing among themselves that very point and he interrupted, "How much more valuable is a man than an animal! Therefore it is lawful to do good on Shabbat." If they did not know before, they knew now that Jesus could keep up with them on arguing and debating as well or better than anyone. He was even using one of their strategies for debating that they used with great frequency. They called it "kal v'homer," or reasoning from the easy to the hard. The way the argument went in this case, if we know we would rescue an animal in distress on Shabbat, then all the more so would we rescue a person. They got so caught up in his question about pulling an animal out of a pit on Shabbat that they did not even think to point out how different this case with the man and the deformed hand was from that. His hand was deformed the day before Shabbat and the day before that, so what was one more day. Jesus was, however, teaching them a much more important lesson than the ability to reason from the easy to the hard. He was teaching them his important lesson that we had to follow the laws of Judaism while paying close attention to what was loving and compassionate. Jesus' big rebuke of the Pharisees was that they had allowed themselves to get too caught up with following the laws, important as that was, and they were forgetting to treat every person with kindness and compassion. And right then, as they were all pondering the lesson he had taught, he had the man hold out his hand and right there, in the middle of Shabbat, in front of everyone, Jesus healed him. The Pharisees were furious and they hated the fact that so many people were enraptured by Jesus' teachings and his ability to bring healing with his forgiveness of sins.

All of us who felt attached to Jesus and were following him, from the closest twelve apostles to those of us outside that inner circle, knew that he often spoke in mysterious and cryptic ways and we could not always understand what he was saying. This even applied to his own family. One day he was addressing a crowd of people, which he did now quite frequently, and someone pulled on his robe and told him, "Your mother and brothers are waiting outside, wanting to speak to you." Rather than stop what he was doing and talking to his family, he said, "Who is my mother and who are my brothers?," and we knew he was not referring to Mary and the men he referred to as his brothers, although we all knew Mary never had any more children. He turned to his apostles and said, "Here are my mother and my brothers. For whoever does the will of my Father in Heaven is my brother and sister and mother." As we had done so often, we just looked at the apostles and then each other. He seemed to be telling us that family was not defined by who was related by blood to you but by who became and would still become a person following God's teachings. Once again he was teaching us, this time about what family really meant.

One day, thinking about such mysterious language, the apostles came to Jesus, as he was telling one of his parables, and they asked him why he keeps talking to people with stories. They insisted on knowing why he did not just tell them the lesson he was trying to teach and not use parables about sowers and reapers and the like. He told the apostles that he used parables because the normal people needed stories to hold onto and that they would not always understand the deeper meaning. The apostles, on the other hand, possessed a gift of understanding and they could hear and understand the greater mysteries of his stories. It seemed to the apostles and to many of the rest of us that he wanted us to struggle to understand the lessons he was teaching and we even had the idea that these parables would be remembered for a long time after we were all gone.

He taught with so many parables though and each time we had to work to understand what he was saying to us. Sometimes it just seemed impossible that we would understand what the teacher was saying to us. We had to struggle to figure out what mustard seeds, pearls and nets represented, the deep and confounding message he was trying to convey. We talked among ourselves and as we discussed the teacher's parables, the meaning and lesson became more and more clear over time, but I'm not sure we ever completely understood.

There were some moments during Jesus' time of teaching and preaching that stood out to us and forced us to wonder who he really was. One of those moments came after an ordinary time of teaching to a crowd on the shores of the sea, as so often happened. Jesus dismissed his apostles and then lingered with the crowd for a while, as he often did, staying to heal a sick child, answer a question and just touch a hand with comfort and consolation. After finally dismissing the crowd he did something else he often did, he wandered off to pray in solitude. Everyone knew to leave him alone during these times, that he was doing what he had urged us to do, to pray to God alone, not just in the congregation at the fixed times of morning, afternoon and evening. By the time his prayers were finished it was late in the afternoon, the winds on the sea were picking up and he came to the shore. The boat with the apostles was already well out to sea. Seemingly without giving it another thought and with some of us sitting on the shore watching it all, he walked out on the water to the apostles' boat. They were terrified and stunned and all of us were speechless and dumfounded. We heard him say, "Take courage. It is I. Do not be afraid." The next thing that happened really struck us as unbelievable. We saw, off in the distance, out on the water, Peter getting out of the boat, walking on the water toward Jesus. Just like that, after taking a few steps, Peter started to sink. Jesus reached out to him and caught him by the hand and we heard him say, "You of little faith, why did you doubt?" They both then climbed into the boat.

We looked at each other on the rock-strewn shore and were stunned at what we had just seen. The apostles later told us that when Jesus and Peter got back into the boat they all declared, "Truly you are the son of God." The apostles were coming to the conclusion that this Jesus, their teacher and leader, was something different from them, a person sent by, directed, even inspired by God. The wonder and amazement of all of us from his closest apostles, to us his followers, to those who just came once to hear him teach was becoming profound and deep. All of us were being forced to confront the question we had pretended to ignore: Who is he?

Chapter 5

Who Is He?

Witnessing all this young man, Jesus of Nazareth, had done and said, all the healings and the wondrous moments of the last months I and so many more were left with a single, probing question: "Who is he?" From our hometown I knew he was the son of Joseph and Mary, although there was still some mystery even about that. He was their son, a child of our town, a boy I had known since infancy and while he always seemed special and out of the ordinary, what was happening now that he was an adult was confounding and even disturbing.

People were ready with every kind of wild story and rumor. Some were suggesting he was John the Baptist resurrected from the dead! There were people speculating he was one of the prophets, even Elijah. Everyone knew Elijah was the prophet who would announce the coming of the messiah, but Jesus was him? We knew he was somehow different, certainly special, but John the Baptist, a prophet or even Elijah just seemed so hard to believe. On the other hand, maybe these things could explain how he could heal people and even maybe walk on the waters of the Galilee. I had to acknowledge that during that fierce and scary storm on the Galilee it was Jesus who made the winds die down and the waves subside. This young man had powers and abilities that no ordinary person possessed and we were left with the troubling and perplexing question, "Who is he?"

I finally went to his disciple who knew him the best, the one everyone turned to when Jesus himself was not around. I approached Peter, whom I knew well by now after all the travels we had taken together with Jesus, and I asked him if we could take a walk. Always agreeable, although sometimes a bit timid, even reticent, he consented to a walk and chat.

"Peter," I blurted out, "I need to know who Jesus is."

"Micah, you have known him longer than any of us, you know Mary and Joseph, you're even family friends, you were there when they came back from Bethlehem and Egypt, he is a friend of your daughter, Rachel. You know who Jesus is."

"Peter, I know all that and we have even celebrated Passover together and I watched him grow up in my own house, in the synagogue and in Nazareth. But now I am not sure I know who he really is."

Peter thought for a while and I watched the birds swoop and swirl overhead. I knew he was trying to figure out an answer to my simple and impossible question. "Micah, we have discussed this among ourselves, believe me. Jesus is reluctant to use a single term to describe who he is. But we did have a pretty important conversation up north at Caesarea Philippi."

Breathlessly, eager to hear every detail, Micah responded, "Tell me everything, it is such a mystery to me after all this."

"Micah," Peter calmly answered, "it might still be a mystery. I'm not sure I even fully understand, but here's what happened. We were at Caesarea Philippi, so beautiful and lush with the headwaters of the Jordan River and Sea of Galilee burbling up from the earth and without any idea of why it was coming up, Jesus asked us, 'Who do people say that I am?' We were stunned and looked at each other. I finally said to him, 'Some say John the Baptist, others say Elijah, and still others, Jeremiah or one of the prophets.' To tell you the truth, Micah, I think he thought I was evading his question. He went on to ask, 'But what about you, who do you say that I am?'"

Peter looked flushed and nervous just recounting the story to me, telling me everything about the conversation. "Micah, I felt a lump in my throat, my heart was pounding in my chest. I had these thoughts but I had never shared them with anyone and certainly not with our teacher, Jesus. I didn't know what to say, but I finally blurted it out: You are the messiah, the Son of the living God."

I could not control my amazement. "You said that to him, that you thought he was the messiah? You actually said that to him? What did he say?"

Peter got really quiet and looked about to make sure no one was listening and whispered, "Jesus said, 'Blessed are you, Simon, son of Jonah, for this was not revealed to you by man, but by my Father in heaven.' He went on to talk about me being Peter, my Greek name, and how he was going to build his church on this rock. It was a play on the meaning of my Greek name, Peter, which means rock, of course. He's going to build a church on me! Micah, I don't even really know what he means."

"Peter, this is remarkable, astounding, I don't even know how to describe it. You tell Jesus that people think he is maybe a resurrected John the Baptist, or Elijah or one of the prophets and then you tell him that you believe he is the messiah! And he pretty much confirms what you believe! How do we make sense of this? What does all this mean?"

"Micah," Peter said softly, as if his loud voice would make it all unreal, "I believe, the apostles believe Jesus is the messiah we have been waiting for. We believe God has anointed him to change everything, to bring about an end to our suffering. This is it, what we have been waiting for all these years."

I was trembling, afraid of the very thoughts I was holding in my heart and mind. "Our people, Israel, has waited for generations for God to anoint a person to rule over us, to change history. On

Passover we yearn for the messiah, at the end of Shabbat we hope for the messiah, in our prayers every day we plead for the messiah and now you believe Jesus, son of Joseph and Mary, the kid who practically grew up in my house playing with my daughter is the one, the anointed one of God?"

I went on and on, now rambling as thoughts rushed to my mind and just as quickly to my mouth, "Shouldn't we tell everyone, go around announcing it, the messiah has come!" Just as quickly and abruptly, Peter stopped me, put his hand out and said, "No, Micah, we cannot. Jesus told us very firmly not to tell anyone."

"But why, if you, if we believe he is the anointed one, why would we not tell anyone? Why would we not tell everyone? This makes no sense." With firmness in his voice that I had only heard a few times before Peter replied, "It is not yet time, Jesus does not want us to talk about it. I think he wants to teach his message, what he wants to tell people about the Kingdom of God without people getting excited about him being the messiah."

"Peter, this is huge, this changes everything. People think he's the resurrected John the Baptist or Elijah announcing the coming of the messiah and instead he **is** the messiah! I don't know what to make of it. When does this Kingdom of God happen? When is Rome thrown out of Israel, when does our oppression end?"

"Micah, we all had the same questions and all he does when we ask is say, 'It is not yet time.' We just have to be patient and wait."

I was reeling with questions, one after another coming to my mind. "Peter, we are living our Jewish lives, keeping kosher, observing Shabbat. Should we still be doing all that if the messiah has arrived? Do our lives go on as they have before or does everything change now?"

"I simply do not know, Micah. Remember that our sages, when they discussed that very question without knowing when the messiah would arrive argued that same point. 'Should we observe Jewish law when the messiah has come?' They did not know the answer and now that the messiah has arrived we still do not know."

"Peter, the messiah is supposed to be a descendant of King David and I remember that Joseph traces his family back to David. So that means Jesus is himself a descendant! Maybe that answers the questions about who he is."

"But remember, Micah, there are now, since it's been a thousand years since King David ruled Israel, thousands of people who can trace their lineage. Those of us with faith in Jesus are happy to know he fulfills that prophecy, but there is so much more for us to consider."

"Peter, there is so much to think about here. I am so confused and amazed and bewildered."

"Micah, after all that and with everything we have witnessed and heard, it all comes down to faith. Each person has to decide if he believes that Jesus is the messiah we have been waiting for."

I offered my hand to Peter and walked off. I had to talk to Shoshanah about all this. I had to know what she thought. She had not seen and heard all I had, at least not directly, but I had told her everything and now we needed to talk, or really, I needed to listen to her.

Her beauty, as always, was captivating and it was like I was seeing her for the first time every time I saw her after being gone for a few weeks. "Shoshanah, it is always so good to see you and feel your touch. I have so much to talk to you about and I need to hear what you think and see if you agree with me or if you think I am crazy or something."

"Micah, slow down, I don't even know what you're talking about and you're going so fast it's hard to keep up with you. What do you need to tell me? Is this about your wanderings with Jesus and what he is saying and doing?"

"Oh, Shoshanah, you don't even know everything I have seen and experienced and what Peter has told me." I told her about the calming of the storm and the healing of lame and deformed people, the blind man who could now see and the person whose deformed hand was now fine. I told her about Jesus walking on the water of the Galilee and even how he had raised a dead man back to life. I went on and on.

"Micah, you know we have heard some of this before, people who can heal the sick because of their intimate relationship with God, people who hear God's voice, the sages who can do amazing things, even heal sick people and raise the dead back to life. Remember even the prophets Elijah and Elisha raised dead people back to life and they were not the messiah."

As frustrating and difficult as it was to hear what Shoshanah was saying, and I had to admit I had considered all these things I still held onto my faith. I was increasingly convinced that Jesus was the messiah we had been waiting for all these generations. It felt like there was no single right answer and all I could do was listen to my heart. My love for Shoshanah as my dear wife and beloved mother of my children did not convince me she was right about Jesus.

I left the conversation with Shoshanah and walked the fields and hills of Nazareth to think and reflect. My wife's reservations about Jesus as the messiah were reasonable and thoughtful and I had to consider them seriously. But she did not see or hear what I have seen and heard and I had to wonder if her ideas about Jesus would be different if she had been a direct witness. This all reminded me of the popular story of the sage who was approached by two people in town in a fierce dispute over one thing or another. The sage sat in his study while his wife sat just outside the door. The first disputant came into the sage's study and yelled and screamed about how the other person had wronged him so terribly. The wife heard her husband say, "You're right!" The second party to the dispute came into the study and yelled just as fiercely, making his case vehemently. The sage's wife heard her husband tell this disputant, "You're right!" She was shocked and stormed into her husband's study. "One person comes in, makes his case and you tell him he's right and then the other person argues just the opposite and you tell him he's right. Which is it? They can't both be right." The rabbi pondered for a moment and said to his wife, "You know, you're right!"

That was exactly how I felt in that moment. When I thought about Jesus being the messiah I was sure I was right and when I talked to Shoshanah and some of the other people in the synagogue who did not believe, I thought they were right. We could not all be right! I was so confused and bewildered and knew this was going to be the spiritual struggle of my life. Could people have faith in Jesus if they had never seen or heard him, if they had never witnessed his miraculous deeds or his profound teachings?

My wanderings took me back to Capernaum where so many of Jesus' apostles and students lived and debated. As soon as I entered town I heard the news—Jesus had decided he was going to Jerusalem! Many people were alarmed and scared, knowing the Sadducees in Jerusalem and the Roman troops were not going to be as tolerant of Jesus as the local Pharisees in the Galilee were. The Pharisees wanted to argue with Jesus, even challenge his authority to do what he was doing and say what he was saying, but the Sadducees and Romans might want to imprison or even kill him. All of his faithful followers were frightened. Jesus insisted that whatever dangers resided in Jerusalem for him, he had to go. He even predicted his own death and then mysteriously suggested he would then be raised back to life on the third day after his death. All of us who loved Jesus were mystified and disturbed by all this and were not sure how to make sense of it. Jesus was the only one completely at peace.

He was even at peace when the dreaded tax collector came. We all tried to avoid the taxes and would have loved to be able to bribe them like the rich people, but we always ended up having to pay. The Jews not only had to pay the Romans taxes but we had the tax for the Temple too. Jesus taught us that he and the apostles were exempt from the taxes because we were now living in the kingdom of God, not men. But when the Temple tax collectors came Jesus instructed Peter to go fishing. In the mouth of the first fish he caught were four coins, enough to pay the taxes for Peter and Jesus. This was just one more lesson about peace and the kingdoms of God and man from our teacher.

Inevitably, as we were all preparing to leave for Jerusalem, nervous about what was to come if we were confronted by the Sadducees or the Romans, Jesus was continuing to teach and to heal. As was so often the case, some Pharisees, looking once again to challenge Jesus on his teaching and authority, confronted him with a test. They asked if it was legal for a man to divorce his wife. They knew full well that the Torah taught (Deuteronomy 24) that one could divorce his wife and they knew that during what we were starting to call the Sermon on the Mount Jesus had taught that divorce was only acceptable in cases of sexual immorality. They challenged him, knowing he was stricter about divorce than scripture was, that the Torah did not specify the grounds for divorce. They wanted to see if they could catch him contradicting the Torah or being inconsistent with his own teachings. What our teacher said to them, citing the time from Creation when God created man and woman was, "So they are no longer two, but one, therefore what God has joined together, let man not separate." Immediately they thought they had him contradicting Torah and threw it in his face that Moses had said one could get a divorce. Jesus calmly and firmly challenged them right back, "Moses permitted you to divorce your wives because your hearts were hard. But it was not this way from the beginning. 'I tell you that anyone who divorces his wife, except for marital unfaithfulness, and marries another woman, commits adultery.'" Some of the apostles concluded from this that it was too hard and they should simply stay unmarried. Jesus turned to them and cryptically suggested, "The one who can accept this should accept it."

Once again we were stunned and while the conversation between Jesus and the Pharisees on this subject and others continued on because they always continued on, most of us were no longer paying attention and the scribes were not even taking notes any more. We were all arguing among ourselves about marriage, divorce, sexual immorality and the prospect of avoiding marriage altogether. I could never imagine not getting married because I loved Shoshanah so, but I suspected that some or all of the apostles were concluding that their commitment to Jesus and his teachings were so strong and marriage was such a huge commitment, that they were just going to stay unmarried.

We had all these weighty subjects to discuss and consider while on the road from Galilee to Jerusalem through Samaria and Judea, and our heads were spinning. The Pharisees never gave up challenging Jesus, trying to question his authority to teach and we never gave up listening to him and loving everything he taught us. Sometimes the Pharisees would be approaching and we would just look at each other and nod our heads, knowing what was coming. I do not think anything they said ever disturbed or even bothered Jesus, I think he saw these as more opportunities to teach.

One day a wealthy young man approached our leader and asked him what he had to do to earn eternal life. We all would have looked at each other and stumbled around for an answer, but of course Jesus immediately rattled off, "Do not murder, do not commit adultery, do not steal, do not give false testimony, honor your father and mother and love your neighbor as yourself." He threw that last one in with the ones from the Ten Commandments because he loved it so. The young man said he had been following all that and needed more direction. Jesus turned to him and instructed him, "Go sell your possessions and give to the poor and you will have treasure in heaven. Then come follow me." The young wealthy man's eyes opened wide, his mouth fell open and he went on to tell Jesus how sad he was because he was so wealthy and it would be impossible to give all he had to the poor and be left with nothing for himself. Jesus put his hand on the young man's shoulders and told him, "It is hard for a rich man to enter the kingdom of heaven. Again, I tell you it is harder for a camel to go through the eye of a needle than for a rich man to enter the kingdom of God." The young man slipped away, apparently not quite ready to give everything away and the apostles were, again as so often before, stunned. They clamored among themselves and I listened in as they speculated on why it would be so difficult for a rich man to enter heaven. Someone suggested it was because the rich man was so devoted to what he had rather than to God. Peter pointed out to Jesus that they had all given up everything, their fishing and farming livelihoods, their families, everything to follow him. I heard Jesus tell him and the others, "Everyone who has left houses or brothers or sisters or father or mother or children or fields for my sake will receive a hundred times as much and will inherit eternal life."

The apostles and those of us not quite among them but following Jesus nonetheless pondered what he had just taught us. So many of us and so many who were not among us were so devoted to our possessions, the things we owned, the fine pottery, the linen clothes as well of course as our families, the people we loved. We concluded that Jesus was telling us that these are not the things that mattered but that his lessons, God's presence in our lives and our love of God is what mattered most. We knew that with every teaching he offered, every message he gave to us he was changing our lives, lifting us beyond where we had been before he was with us. We knew our lives would never be the same now that his words were in our heart and spirit.

One of the most devoted of Jesus' followers, although not regarded as an apostle was Mary from the town of Magdal on the shores of the Sea of Galilee. She was so tender with Jesus, making it clear she loved him, not as a woman loves a man, but as a devoted student loves her teacher. She reminded us all, when we got frustrated or angry at some provocation from non-believers, that Jesus was teaching us to love everyone, even those who challenged us. She was a great support to him and all of us.

Suddenly and so disturbingly, along the road to Jerusalem, Jesus crushed us. Seemingly out of nowhere, as we were approaching the holy city and could almost see the spires of the Herodian Temple, Jesus took the twelve apostles aside from the rest of us. This happened occasionally, not too often, and those of us who were not apostles knew this meant he had to say something important and maybe even troubling. It was hours later before the apostles started to share with us how he had described that once they entered Jerusalem the Sadducees would accost him and hand him over to the Romans. Then they quoted him exactly, "They will condemn the Son of Man to death and will turn him over to the Gentiles to be mocked and flogged and crucified. On the third day he will be raised to life."

Each man turned to the other and realized we all had tears in our eyes and could not believe what we had just heard. We were about to enter Jerusalem willingly, even eagerly, led by our teacher and he knew or believed or predicted, it was hard for us to know which it was, that he would be turned over to the Romans who would mock him, torture him and kill him. To a man we knew it was futile to try to persuade Jesus to turn back, to return to the peace and quiet of the Galilee where only the rhetorical taunts and challenges of the Pharisees could concern us. No words passed among us but each one of us dearly wished we could find some words that would convince Jesus not to enter Jerusalem, this burning cauldron of danger, threat and death. There were no such words and there was no way other than forward, up the hills to Jerusalem. I was, simply, terrified.

Chapter 6

Jesus Takes His Ministry to Jerusalem

None of us from Nazareth or the rest of Galilee knew Jerusalem very well and what we knew was scary. We knew the Sadducees in the holy city ruled the Jewish community with an iron hand permitted them by the Romans. We knew the real power was Rome and that Rome insisted on things staying tranquil and quiet. What they had made clear over the years was that they would not tolerate any disturbance, anything that even sounded like a mob, anything that could conceivably percolate into a rebellion or uprising. The Roman army in Jerusalem operated at the behest of the prefect, Pontius Pilate, and he was a tyrant. He allowed for no disturbances or uprisings and operated on the principle that all tyrants did — if there is any sign of an uprising, you assassinate the leader, massacre the followers or do both. Pilate used his army freely and willingly and many were assassinated and massacred in the name of keeping the peace. Pilate was ruthless. He allowed the Sadducees to have their Sanhedrin, a ruling council, only to the extent that they supported his insistence on keeping the peace. If they failed at this task they knew he would simply massacre them and find others to replace them. One could look long and hard and with futility to find any compassion in the rule of Pontius Pilate. All of us knew his reputation and how well-earned it was. We were very afraid.

The Jews and the Romans knew that messianic expectations among us Jews were at a fever pitch during the rule of Pilate. We felt oppressed for good reason and could not imagine any end to Roman oppression except by the intercession of God's anointed one. We believed and prayed for the messiah and fully expected that the first and most important consequence of his long-awaited appearance was to end the oppression of the Jews in the Land of Israel. To us that quite simply meant the destruction of Roman rule in Jerusalem and the rest of Israel. Rome was not going anywhere willingly from this strategic position at the crossroads of Africa, Asia and Europe. They ruled the region with an iron hand and knew that the Jews had what the Romans regarded as a fantasy of some person the God of the Jews would anoint and that the anointed one would liberate the people from Roman rule.

While the Romans did not truly fear any Jewish claimant to the messianic throne, they knew that anyone claiming to be this anointed one would by necessity lead an army of some sort against Rome. At least, that had always been the case before. While they did not fear any Jewish uprising they also had no reason to wait until it got stronger and stronger and more difficult to crush. Rome took every sign of uprising and rebellion seriously and they would not hesitate to destroy with great violence the people involved as soon as they saw the first signs of a movement. By the time Jesus entered Jerusalem with his following from Galilee Pilate had already massacred hundreds of people and assassinated several leaders of other real or imagined uprisings whom he deemed a threat. Pilate had no intention of tolerating any mob that even sounded like a rebellion and the very word messiah was a signal to him that a rebellion was getting started.

As Jewish followers of Jesus we knew all this about Pilate and the Romans and it was this reality that frightened us about Jesus' plan to come to Jerusalem. Everything was so quiet and uplifting in Galilee where crowds could gather to see and hear Jesus, he could teach all of us about the kingdom of God and we could come to him for healing and the expulsion of evil spirits. I remembered thinking that the worst thing we had to worry about then was the Pharisees and their challenges to Jesus and his authority. That was nothing compared to what we were about to face in Jerusalem with the Sadducees and Romans.

After the long and tiring ascent up the hills east of Jerusalem we finally approached what we knew was the Mt. of Olives from the east. Since it was springtime, almost Passover, the hills were greener than usual with shrubs and even wild flowers. At no other time than this were these hills more beautiful than they were now but it was still a difficult hike up from the Jordan Valley. The sun was hot and we were thirsty and terrified all at the same time. Jesus sent two of the apostles ahead and gave them instructions to find a donkey for him to ride into the city. This was not going to be a quiet entry into the cauldron of Jerusalem, Jesus was going to enter as a triumphant king of Israel. I knew inside my heart that I was not convinced of the wisdom of his plan but he was going to go ahead as he chose.

The gray donkey approached us and the apostles threw some cloaks over him so Jesus could ride. Exultant apostles could not contain themselves, believing all this was in fulfillment of the scriptural passage (Zechariah 9) about the king of Israel entering Jerusalem on a donkey. Our sages had always understood this grand entrance was going to be for a new king to rule over Israel like David had, but in these anxious and tense years many of us had come to believe the king would actually be the awaited messiah as king of our people. Some were whooping and hollering and Jesus only had to look at them with that stern look of his to quiet them down. People were throwing down tree branches to ease his ride and some were singing, hailing him as "Son of David," suggesting they believed he was the messiah for whom we had prayed and longed all these years.

Approaching Jerusalem from the east, approaching the gate of the city that would give us entrance to the holy places of our people, Jesus, the donkey and the crowd entered and we could feel the excitement of the city. We could not imagine anything as grand and spectacular as this holy city and the magnificent Temple that bestrode it all. Even in such a magnificent and huge city people had heard something big was going on, that this Jesus from Galilee was approaching. Whether people knew who this person was or not, they knew there was great anticipation about his approach and they also knew the Romans were tensely holding their spears and shields, seeming to squeeze them harder and harder, eager to use them at a moment's notice if the officers deemed it necessary. People were at their doorways and gathering in the streets to see the sight of a lonely Jew, surrounded by crowds, but somehow in his own solitude, riding a donkey that proclaimed his status as a descendant of David, king of Israel, the awaited messiah of the

Jewish people. Some people believed he was a prophet, very different from messiah and that was more my belief but the one thing I was sure about was that I was not so sure one way or the other.

All of us, Jesus, his apostles, the growing crowds and folks like me went straight from the entrance into Jerusalem to the Temple itself. It had never looked as glorious in the brilliant spring sunshine as it did this spectacular day. We could tell the Romans were tense, fidgeting with their spears and shields, some looking like they were just waiting to do some killing. Those of us who noticed could not help but be frightened while at the same time excited about the entry to Jerusalem. When we got to the outer courtyards of the Temple there was the usual commotion and tumult, people selling things, the money changers turning people's local currency into Roman currency for Jerusalem, animals flying and running around in a frenzy. It was as if the animals knew they were about to be offered up to our God in fulfillment of scriptural commands. There was so much noise and the smells were horrendous and it just seemed like so much chaos, nothing like the quiet of Nazareth or even Capernaum. Suddenly there was screaming and shrieking that broke through all the tumult that caught everyone's attention. I made my way forward through the pushing and shoving crowds and saw Jesus at the center of it, turning tables over and shouting. "My house will be called a house of prayer but you are making it a den of robbers." We figured out that he was upset about the money changers on Temple grounds and while someone had to convert people's currency it did not have to be right there. Jesus was enraged and frustrated at the commerce being done where people were supposed to be making sacrificial offerings and praying to God. As was so often the case he did not seem to worry much about the consequences because he had this fierce devotion to God and service to God that compelled him to act when others might be timid. In another familiar scene, people who could not walk or see came to him for healing but now the Sadducee priests and teachers were watching and frowning. When they heard the chants of "Son of David" they were really upset and arguing among themselves about who this Jesus was claiming to be. Serenely and with dignity he quite simply walked out of the Temple courtyard.

I grabbed James, son of Zebedee, one of the apostles, a man I had always found to be honest and willing to talk openly about Jesus and his own faith. "James, what are we to make of all this, how do we understand Jesus' willingness to come to Jerusalem and face the Sadducees and Romans? What do you make of his willingness to die but also his rage at the corrupt commercial activities of the money changers at the Temple?"

"Micah, you have to remember that while we revere Jesus and consider him different than all of us, somehow closer to God than all of us, he is still

Jesus from Nazareth. He is fully devoted to God the father and brings His presence into our lives, and at the same time he is the same person we have always known, whom you have known since he was a baby. He is willing to die if that is what must come, but he also is furious when people lose their focus on serving God and loving God."

"James, I am so confused and I often feel lost in all this. I am older than all of you, but you all seem so much more sure about your faith than I am. I don't know what to believe anymore."

"Micah," James replied, with his hand on my shoulder as he often did, "all I can tell you is to listen to your heart, be present for what Jesus teaches us and what he does. Open your heart."

He knew I was struggling and wanting to have his faith and that of the other apostles. He also had the wisdom to know that I had to arrive at that faith on my own. So much was happening and I could not figure it all out.

Just the next day James rushed up to me, breathless and asked me if I remembered our conversation from the previous day about my struggles with faith. How could I not remember, the words kept echoing in my mind and spirit, my struggle was far from over. He said, "Then let me share a story from this very morning." I was, of course, eager to hear what had him so excited.

"Jesus was on his way back to Jerusalem and of course after the tumultuous day past he had forgotten to eat and now he was famished. He told us how he had approached a lovely fig tree, hoping to have some figs for breakfast and the tree had plenty of leaves and no figs to eat. He told us that he turned to the tree and said to it, 'May you never bear fruit again!' When he told us the story we insisted on hearing how the tree had withered in a moment. He turned to us in that way he had when he was desperate for us to understand something we had not fully understood and quietly said, "I tell you the truth, if you have faith, and do not doubt, not only can you do what was done to the fig tree, but also you can say to this mountain, 'Go throw yourself into the sea', and it will be done. If you believe, you will receive whatever you ask for in prayer.' We were, again, stunned."

"What does it all mean?" I asked. "Jesus curses a fig tree and it withers and I'm supposed to believe that if I, Micah, pray for something it will happen? I have so much difficulty believing it."

"Precisely," James responded. "Our faith, mine, yours, that of the apostles, is still not strong enough. I don't think it's about making a tree wither but about praying and believing with fervor and strength. Jesus needs us to have faith and our faith is too weak. Your faith, Micah, is too weak. It is not our arms that must be stronger but our faith."

I knew what James meant, I knew what Jesus desired for me, for all of us, but it was so hard. Maybe it had to be difficult, maybe faith could never be easy. I loved James for doing this and I loved the story and the lesson Jesus was teaching and I knew my faith needed to be stronger, I just did not know how or when that was going to happen.

Later that day Jesus again entered the Temple grounds and once again everyone was tense and nervous. I could see it in the eyes of the Jerusalem residents, all too familiar with uprisings, with mobs following a charismatic leader, with religious leaders claiming to be the messiah. They were all too familiar with the inevitable Roman crackdown, the massacres, the blood in the streets, the death to anyone standing too close or running too slow to avoid their swords. Their eyes were asking us if this was going to be one more tragedy of blood and death. All we could do is share with them our faith, imperfect as it was, our resolve, shaky as it was and our hope, which was fervent and undying.

Once we were all, including Jesus, in the Temple courtyards it seemed the elders, the officials, the priests did not wait a moment before pouncing on Jesus and challenging him. They were ready for dispute and confrontation and we could see them all looking smugly at each other, sure they were finally going to be able to expose him as the fraud they believed him to be. They just knew that if they could show the adoring crowds how inauthentic he was the people would melt away and turn back to their families and their businesses and farms. This was the Sadduceean elite leadership of Israel, placed in their lofty positions by the ruling Romans and they were certain they would be successful where the weak Pharisees in Galilee could not. They knew they had to quiet these wild crowds following him everywhere or the Romans would do what they had done so often. This Jesus had to be neutralized and marginalized, and if necessary they would have to find a way to dispose of him.

As soon as he entered the city in the morning the Sadducee priests and elders challenged him on his authority, questioning by what authority he was saying and doing the things he was doing that were contrary to their understanding of Jewish law. Jesus knew better than to answer their question simply and directly because they would find a way to use it against him. Summoning his dignity and integrity he paused for a moment and asked them about John the Baptist, "John's baptism, where did it come from? Was it from heaven or man?"

The priests and elders shuffled their feet, looked at each other and knew right away they were about to walk into a trap. They knew that if they answered that John's authority came from heaven the question would be why they did not believe him. They also knew that if they said it came from man then it would sound like they were afraid of the masses who followed him and how could they ignore the wishes and faith of the people? With weakness and their usual lack of character they mumbled, "We don't know."

Jesus smiled just a bit and said, "In that case, I'm not going to answer your question either." With that he walked off to teach and lead the people. He taught them, as he had in Galilee, with parables that were not always perfectly clear to the people but which the apostles could explain to them since they were more accustomed to his parables. He was always trying to get the people to understand that if they had faith in him they would know the kingdom of God and that if they lacked in faith they would never know the kingdom.

As for me, Micah, a simple olive merchant from Nazareth, having faith in Jesus as a teacher, as a man intimate with God, a man who could somehow lead us to the kingdom of God was pretty easy. I believed in him and his message. It was only when people started talking about him as the promised anointed one, the messiah, that I struggled, as Shoshanah and I had discussed. Here in Jerusalem everything was heightened, everyone seemed to be tense and on edge, every moment seemed fraught with danger and suspense. These confrontations with Jesus came one after the other and each time we wondered when one of the priests or elders would lash out verbally or physically.

One of the Sadducees confronted Jesus with the convoluted situation in which a married man dies without having any children, so his unmarried brother had to marry the widow, according to the law in Deuteronomy 25. In their improbable case each of seven brothers died in succession without impregnating the wife and finally she died. Their question: at the resurrection, to which of the seven brothers would she be married since she had been married to each in his own turn? With their smug glances and proud faces it was clear they were sure they had stumped Jesus. The teacher responded as he always did, quietly, gently and with dignity, first pointing out that they do not know scripture or God's power. He went on to instruct them, "At the resurrection people will neither marry nor be given in marriage; they will be like the angels in heaven." He continued to explain that God is the God of the living not the dead and they should not focus on death so much. They finally fell in silence, having been taught by the teacher.

I loved being part of these discussions and hearing what Jesus told the people questioning him, not least because it was so inspiring to see how Jesus maintained his composure. He taught the Pharisee questioners that the greatest laws of Scripture were to love the Lord your God with all your heart and soul and mind and also to love your neighbor as yourself. He insisted that everything else in Scripture depended on these two teachings about love. He did not talk about dietary laws or Shabbat observance or festivals or sacrificial offerings but about how we are commanded to love each other and God. What could be more profound, even simpler than that, just to love God and each other.

Jesus finally found a way to silence the critics and end the fruitless and futile questioning. He asked the Pharisees whose son the messiah would be and they insisted, as their teaching had always held, that he would be the son of David. Citing Psalm 110 he argued that the messiah would be the son of God. Everyone around him was stunned into silence and that exchange put an end to all the verbal confrontations. What we could not know is that the confrontations would soon turn physical.

The teacher continued to keep teaching of course. He taught about what he regarded as the hypocrisy of the Pharisees, their focus on adherence to their leadership and the laws rather than on the kingdom of God. He reached out to the people, trying to convince them that the Pharisees did not have their interests at heart and they could not keep the focus of the people on God and His kingdom. Jesus was certain that people needed to pay less attention to punctilious adherence to the laws of Moses and more on their love of God and each other. He taught the people that the grand buildings of the Temple and all the glory of the priests and the exacting offerings of animals and grains could not bring them closer to God or the end of days. He insisted to all of us, the apostles and other followers, that the end of days, while uncertain and unknowable was something about which we had to be vigilant and watchful. We could not dare to lose our focus on things like temples and priests and laws but should be watching for, waiting for the end days God has promised.

After all these important teachings that had our heads reeling with the kingdom of God and the end days and resurrection, Jesus brought his apostles back to the realities of the calendar and the momentous events that were coming very soon. He reminded them that the Passover festival was only two days away and that the Romans were going to take him and execute him on the cross. First the apostles and then the rest of us who were close to Jesus had to know that the Sadducees were going to arrest him and turn him over to the Romans. Passover usually came to us with joy and anticipation of great moments of remembrance and offerings but this year we were filled with dread and fear for what our teacher had told us was about to unfold.

Chapter 7

Arrest and Death

Every one of us, each disciple, each follower, each student, every one of us felt a cold gripping fear as the anticipated end drew near. Every one of us except Jesus. He was at peace with everything. He never appeared frightened or shaky. He knew he was soon to be arrested, he knew he would be persecuted and hurt and he knew he would be executed on the Roman cross. He knew that for him, the approach of Passover meant the end of his time with us and the beginning of his suffering, pain and death. And while even he wished there was another way, he was at peace with it all. We were distraught and he saw our grief as expressions of our lack of faith. Our teacher urged us, again and again, to have faith that God's kingdom was coming and that we should not focus on the momentary suffering he was about to endure or the sadness we would feel at his death. Jesus knew no fear about what he had told us was to come but he did have frustration and I think even disappointment that we felt fear and grief at the thought of his anticipated death.

What we did not know was that it would be one of Jesus' twelve apostles, one of the people closest to him, one of those he trusted the most, who would expose and identify him to the Romans. Judas Iscariot, always one of the quietest of the apostles, a man who seemed always to hold back from the crowd, to separate himself from the other apostles was about to betray Jesus. He went to the chief priests and asked how he would be compensated for exposing Jesus to the priests' and Romans' soldiers and guards. In a moment that was reminiscent of Joseph's brothers selling him for coins, Judas sold Jesus for silver. Judas should have been watching out for Jesus, helping our teacher and instead he was conspiring with his adversaries for money. When we learned about this betrayal we were all shocked…all of us but Jesus, who as always was calm and undisturbed by the turn of events. It was as if he knew how things were going to unfold and took it all with a sense of peace and acceptance.

Jesus had, after all, taught us about the imminent approach of the end times, of the approach of God's kingdom. He warned us about future false reports of sightings of him and he implored us not to follow them. He assured us that the very cosmos, the sun and moon would tell us of the arrival of the Son of Man. The problem is that we could not know, desperate as we might be, what the day would be. Only God can know such things. He insisted we be vigilant and used various metaphors and images to implore us to be watchful. He must have had the sense that we would lose our focus and pay attention to other things. He knew us better than we knew ourselves. He taught us that when the Son of Man does return everything will change, nations will gather together and there will be a reckoning of sins.

Finally, Passover came with the darkening sky. Other Jews prepared for a joyous festival, making sure their offerings were ready for the festival, making sure they had the ritual foods prepared. All of us who loved Jesus and followed him and especially the apostles greeted the holiday with some amount of trepidation. Some of the events I will describe here I learned about from the apostles who were present with him during these final hours. They shared with the rest of us what these tragic and tumultuous times were like for Jesus and for them.

The Passover dinner they told me about was momentous in so many ways and ended in tragedy for the apostles and all of us who heard about it later. After finding a place to hold the supper they sat down to offer the blessings, eat the ritual foods, including unleavened bread (matza), bitter herbs, parsley, wine and the lamb they had slaughtered just before the meal. Suddenly Jesus told them that someone was going to reveal him to the Romans. Everyone looked at his neighbor suspiciously and with sadness. These were such difficult times and now everyone was learning about what Judas was doing with the Romans.

We were all furious and again, Jesus was calm. I heard from the apostles that some of them wanted to grab Judas right there and pummel him and Jesus would not let them. He knew that Judas was betraying him because these events had to happen, because all this had to happen to bring about the end times and the coming of the Son of Man. I learned from the apostles that as usual, they could not be as accepting as Jesus was and they could only look to each other and wonder who the betrayer was. Finally Judas spoke up and asked if Jesus thought it was him, trying to deny it at the same time. Jesus calmly and resolutely let Judas know that he knew Judas was the one.

At that point in the dinner the most dramatic moment happened, a moment that would resonate for all of us for years to come. Taking the unleavened bread in his hand he turned to the apostles, offered the blessing over the bread, "Blessed are You, Lord, Sovereign of the universe, who brings forth bread from the earth." Then he broke the unleavened bread and gave each disciple a piece, saying, "Take and eat; this is my body." The apostles all knew, of course, that matza in our Jewish tradition represented the hurried departure of our ancestors from slavery in Egypt over a thousand years ago. They knew, as all of us Jews knew, that the matza has always represented our people's salvation from suffering and slavery and a reminder for us to consider the suffering and slavery of all people in our own times. Now Jesus was telling the apostles and presumably all of us that the bread was, or represented, his body, that somehow he was our new salvation from suffering and slavery.

He did not stop there. He took the cup of wine, the wine that in Judaism always represented our joy and he declared, "Drink from it, all of you. This is my blood of the covenant, which is poured out for many for the forgiveness of sins." He went on to tell the apostles that he would only drink the wine next in his father's kingdom. The apostles were all stunned and a bit perplexed. We associated the blood of the covenant with the circumcision of baby boys, the ceremony we knew as brit, or covenant. The blood of the covenant was the blood first shed by Abraham to represent his and his descendants' covenant with God. We struggled to understand what Jesus was teaching us when he said that this wine was now his blood of the covenant and how it served for the forgiveness of sins. It was clear to all of us that we would have to

127

continue the journey to understand what Jesus was teaching us about the bread and the wine, the body and the blood. However the apostles and then the rest of us understood and would come to understand what Jesus was saying to us, it was very clear that this moment was the pivotal moment of the Passover meal the apostles had with Jesus.

One of the apostles told me about a confounding moment during the supper, when Jesus anticipated that Peter, of all people, was going to deny him during the difficulties and confrontations with Rome and the priests of the Temple. It seems Jesus told the apostles that they would distance themselves from him after his death, perhaps to save their own lives. Peter insisted he would never abandon Jesus and Jesus told Peter that not only would Peter deny him, but he would deny him three times. Peter and the other apostles could not believe what they were hearing and every one of them insisted he would never abandon Jesus.

As usual, Jesus knew exactly what he was talking about. We all had trouble, when we heard about it, believing that Peter of all people could disown Jesus to save his own life. Peter was the disciple closest to Jesus, the one Jesus had said his church would be built on like a solid, unmoving rock. We all knew that Peter was the closest of any disciple or follower of Jesus and it was difficult to believe he would deny Jesus. These times were so difficult and we were being asked to accept inconceivable, incomprehensible ideas and concepts.

The apostles told us about a remarkably poignant moment that night of the Passover dinner between Jesus and three of the apostles, Peter, James and John. They were his closest confidants, the ones he always turned to for counsel and support. All the apostles were resting in the Garden of Gethsemane, a garden of ancient olive trees on the hillside of the Mt. of Olives, facing Jerusalem from the east. Peter, James and John could tell that Jesus was unusually distressed, in a state of turmoil he did not usually reveal to others, even the other apostles. He needed their comfort and loving presence during what was certainly a stressful time, even for him. James later told me that after revealing the state of his soul to these three, he fell to the ground and prayed. They realized he was praying to God that if it was possible for his fate to be reversed, if he could somehow avoid the approaching suffering and death, he would welcome what he called, "this cup," to be taken away. In typical fashion he then declared in his prayer that if this was his Father's will he would willingly accept it.

Apparently after this powerful moment with Peter, James and John they all returned to the other apostles in the garden and the apostles were asleep! Jesus was very disappointed, even angry, as angry as he ever got. He firmly and resolutely told Peter that he expected the men to stay awake during these demanding hours, that they must remain vigilant.

The worst part was that he went away again, this time alone, prayed again and when he returned to the men, he found them sleeping once more. If things could get even worse they did, because after finding them asleep he left a third time and once more they had fallen asleep. For one of the rare moments in his life he actually shouted at the apostles, reprimanding them with harsh words, "Are you still sleeping and resting? Look, the hour is near, and the Son of Man is betrayed into the hands of sinners. Rise, let us go! Here comes the betrayer." Only then did they all notice that Judas was not with them. They knew who the betrayer was, the one Jesus had spoken of during the Passover supper and they have told me that they were not that surprised since he had always hung out on the edges of the group, even when it was just the twelve of them with Jesus.

In the very moment when he said that the betrayer was coming Judas appeared in the garden with guards of the high priest armed with swords and clubs. It seemed like an entire mob was there to apprehend him. All of a sudden, Judas walked right up to Jesus and kissed him on the cheek. The apostles looked to each other and quickly realized this was a signal to the armed men that Jesus was the one for whom they had come. Judas greeted Jesus and Jesus calmly and serenely said, "Friend, do what you came for."

As the armed guards came forward to arrest Jesus one of the apostles—in the frantic pace of the moments no one was quite sure who it had been—rushed forward, reaching for his own sword. Jesus turned and firmly said to the disciple, "Put your sword back in its place." He cryptically explained to all of us, ignoring the mob accosting him, that this was the moment when God was fulfilling His word to Jesus, fulfilling the words of scripture. He said it had to happen just as it was happening and we were wrong and futile to resist. He surely did not want any violence and most certainly not on his behalf. It seems all the apostles then stepped back, recognizing once again that Jesus' faith in the Lord was so much greater than their own. He taught them that violence only breeds more violence and that those who live by the sword will die by the sword.

Those of us who were not at the dinner or at the arrest at the Garden of Gethsemane on the Mount of Olives heard about it later. We were as distressed as the apostles themselves. We wanted to form what would have been an angry mob and take up clubs and swords to fight the soldiers of the priests and the Romans. The apostles taught us what Jesus had taught them, that no one could engage in violence on his behalf, that such an act would be the ultimate betrayal of his ministry. We were left with such anger and burning frustration and there was nothing we could do. We were in Jerusalem, the home of the priests and the Romans and they possessed all the power. We were quite literally powerless to do anything to change Jesus' fate, not least because he did not want us to do anything to help him.

Once word of Jesus' arrest had spread through Jerusalem the city was on edge and tense. Those Jews who supported him and those who did not were arguing with each other, screaming epithets against each other and some actual fights broke out. It seems everyone in Jerusalem had an opinion and was sure he or she was right. We had no idea what was going on outside Jerusalem, and it was probably nothing because they knew nothing of what was going on, but those of us in the city were seething. His followers were enraged with the priests and the Romans that they would arrest and potentially even execute a gentle teacher who threatened no one. His opponents insisted his teachings against the status quo, the suggestions he was the messiah and thus the anticipated one who would overthrow Roman rule in Israel were a threat to their safety and security. They believed he and his movement would only bring about Roman retribution, that all Rome cared about was the avoidance of uprisings and disturbances and he was leading an uprising. His opponents just wanted to continue with their quiet and safe lives and avoid Roman massacres in the face of what they, rightly or wrongly saw as civil disturbances.

Soon we heard new reports, this time from Peter himself. Who could be a better person to recount what had happened than Jesus' closest disciple, Peter, the rock on whom Jesus' church would be built, the rock upon whom many of us, myself included, depended. He came to many of us, apostles and followers, looking ashen and downcast. We all clamored around him to hear what he had to say. He was usually soft-spoken and calm and this time he was quieter than usually and deeply troubled by what he had to share. He told us that Jesus had been taken to the High Priest, Caiaphas. As soon as he said that we all murmured to each other because we knew how stern Caiaphas could be, and also that he was most certainly loyal to Rome, since he could only serve as High Priest as long as he did Rome's bidding to keep things quiet. Peter started to talk, "Jesus was brought to Caiaphas and the other Sadducees and elders were there in the courtyard. I got as close as I could so I could hear the proceedings. There were all kinds of false testimony lodged against Jesus and none of it was sufficient for the Sadducees to convict Jesus of blasphemy. Finally," Peter slowly and quietly continued, "Caiaphas flat out asked Jesus if he was the messiah." We all clamored with one voice, "What did our teacher say?" Except for those who had been at Caesarea Phillipi, we had never heard Jesus talk about being messiah, but we knew Peter believed it and many others did.

"Jesus simply said, 'Yes, it is as you say.' That was it, simply an affirmation that Caiaphas was right." Peter looked to each one of us and said, "Remember this moment—our teacher told the high priest that the claim that he was the messiah was correct!" We were, simply, stunned. The apostles seemed less stunned than the rest of us, they seemed to be used to the idea of Jesus as the messiah, but for the rest of us that was new and even, for some, a bit alarming. At the very least, it explained why the Sadducees and Romans were so upset about Jesus and his movement. The messiah was expected to bring about an end to foreign subjugation, among other things. That most certainly meant an end to Roman rule in Israel. Religiously it meant the fulfillment of what Daniel in scripture and other writings since Daniel had anticipated. A messiah would come to inaugurate an end to history, an end to all suffering and to our ultimate union with God. Was Jesus the messiah he was now openly claiming to be? He told the priests that he was and now we all had to come to our own faith in who he really was.

Peter went on to report more about this momentous confrontation between Jesus and the priests. Caiaphas apparently insisted this was the blasphemy with which Jesus had been charged. We all thought this was odd, because we understood blasphemy was not claiming to be the messiah, whether accurate or not, but that blasphemy was denial and rejection of God. Jesus was by no means doing that when he was stating he was the messiah. Surely the priests were looking for a charge of blasphemy and rushed to make the charge against Jesus so they could get rid of him and his followers. They went on, according to Peter, to mock and mistreat Jesus, even slapping him and spitting on him. We were all disgusted by their hypocrisy and their callousness.

At this point in the retelling, Peter got even more somber and spoke in hushed terms. "I was confronted by a servant girl," he told us, "and she told me she knew I was with Jesus. My chest tightened, I felt acid rise in my throat and," he said haltingly and in a whisper, "I told her I did not know what she was talking about. I went out of the courtyard and repeated the lie, that I did not know Jesus. I even took an oath and said a third time that I did not know Jesus. I am so ashamed. After I denied him the third time a rooster crowed and I remembered Jesus' saying that I would disown him three times. At the time I did not believe him, but here it had turned out to be true." He told us he went out alone, filled with shame and self-loathing and cried bitter tears.

Reports of Jesus being handed over by the priests to the Romans made sense to us in an odd and perverse way. The Sadducees may have wanted him killed to keep things quiet, to crush any talk of him being the messiah, but they had no power to actually do it. The Romans would never allow Jews to execute anyone, even someone claiming to be the messiah. So he was handed over to the Roman authorities and we were all pretty sure what was coming next. In the meantime we got word that Judas, the disciple who had revealed Jesus to the guards coming to arrest him, was filled with remorse. We were glad he felt bad about what he had done, but his feeling bad did not change anything. Apparently he then returned the silver coins the priests had paid him and went out and hung himself. We all responded with a "good riddance" and then felt guilty because we knew that was not how Jesus would have wanted us to respond. One of the followers even pointed out that Judas Iscariot reminded him of Ahitophel, the aide who had been loyal to King David and then joined David's son, Absalom's revolt. Ahitophel betrayed David much as Judas had betrayed Jesus and Ahitophel went out and killed himself just like Judas had just done. We were all reminded that Jesus had told the apostles during what we were starting to call The Last Supper, that one of the apostles would betray him. What eerie parallels we were seeing and experiencing.

Jesus was then brought before Pontius Pilate, the Roman governor. Pilate was the Roman prefect for Judea, the southern region of Israel and he was well known for his brutality, his propensity for executing anyone who he believed was threatening the tranquility of Roman rule. We Jews all feared Pilate, even the Sadducees who held their positions feared Pilate because he wanted them to keep the Jews under control. They knew that the moment Pilate believed they were not keeping the Jews quiet he would have them executed and replace them with others. We saw Jesus before Pilate, standing tall and strong despite the abuse he had taken from the Roman soldiers. Repeating the charges of the priests, Pilate asked Jesus if he was claiming to be the king of the Jews. This seemed to be his understanding of what being the messiah meant.

Jesus repeated what he had told the priests, "Yes, it is as you say."

Then there was this disturbing moment that all of us found so curious. He seemed to claim that there was some custom of releasing a prisoner every year at Passover. We found it odd because none of us could remember any time he had released prisoners. Now he faced the crowd gathering at his palace and shouted out that he would release one prisoner, either the common criminal, Barabas or the man claiming to be the king of the Jews, Jesus. We had never heard of Barabas but none of us could miss the mystery of his Aramaic name which means "son of the father." Could this be a cruel joke of Pilate, putting forth Barabas, "son of the father," with Jesus whom many of us knew as the "Son of man." In any case, he had faced us with a choice, real or false, we could not know with Pilate. A shout rose up from the crowd, from so many who had rejected Jesus, those who feared the wrath of Rome if Jesus survived and succeeded and they yelled, "Crucify him, crucify him." It was clear they were talking about Jesus, not Barabas. They had no fear of Barabas, but with Jesus there was the overriding fear of the wrath of Rome. The crowd shouted, over and over, "Crucify him, crucify him." Pilate had a look of cruel satisfaction on his face. We were sure. He taunted the crowd, turning to a bowl of water only two steps away and washed his hands, declaring his innocence of the death of Jesus. He insisted, against the facts, that it would not be the Romans who would execute him, that somehow the Jews, fearful of Rome and its wrath, were responsible for his death. His thinking was so convoluted none of us could understand it, but we knew it was the workings of Pilate's distorted mind.

In that very moment a new shout arose from the crowd, "Let his blood be on us and on our children." Those of us listening could not even fathom what they meant by this and why they were taking responsibility for the acts of Rome. We had to accept this as one of the mysteries of this incredibly powerful and mysterious moment. We would have to leave this to future generations to understand.

Pilate went ahead, to the amazement of all of us, and released the criminal Barabas to what fate we did not know. Our attention was immediately drawn to the scene of the Roman soldiers whipping Jesus. I could not believe my eyes and like most of my friends I wept at the scene of his dignified suffering. He never cried out, never asked for them to stop, he just took the suffering and pain that was so cruelly imposed this beloved man, our teacher. We came to understand later that the soldiers then took him inside Pilate's residence and abused him even more, seeking to humiliate him. What they did not know was that he could not be humiliated. We, his friends, followers and apostles could be distressed, shaken and disturbed because our faith was weak, but nothing could bring him to his knees.

The Lord was in his heart and he knew that what was happening had to happen. They were the ones made smaller by trying to make him suffer. He only grew larger and greater as they whipped him, spit on him and put a cynical crown of thorns on his head. We despised the Romans for what they were doing to him and even that we knew our own distress was a sign of our own weakness. He would want us to forgive them for what they were doing.

The crowds gathered on the streets of Jerusalem, some out of curiosity at the scene that was being created, some because we loved him and supported him and others because they were happy about the coming crucifixion. As seemed always to be the case, the Jews were divided among ourselves about what we believed. Huge crowds of all kinds of people with different beliefs about Jesus gathered at Golgotha, the hillside outside the city that looked like a skull. Those of us who loved Jesus needed to drown out the jeers of his critics and we needed to combat the idle curiosity of those who did not seem to care one way or the other. We did this for us more than him because even while walking through the streets of the city, bleeding and clearly in pain, he only stumbled under the weight of the Roman cross, not because of any reaction of the crowds. We wept while we watched him approach Golgotha, and he remained, even through the blood, serene and dignified.

Even with us, his followers and friends trying to protect him, the taunts and jeers of his critics, including those of the priests themselves, could be heard. There were taunts from the robbers who were being crucified on either side of him. The priests ridiculed him with shouts that if he were truly the messiah he should save himself now. They insisted that if he had saved others as we all knew he had, that he would surely save himself now. They did not understand, they simply could not or would not understand his submission, his acceptance of his fate, the role his death would play for those who believed in him. How sad we were, in part for their blindness but more for our teacher's pain and suffering. There was among us just this deep, dark and profound sadness at all of it.

The very cosmos cried out at this injustice. Suddenly darkness descended on Golgotha and we could not see each other. In retrospect, some of us recalled the ninth plague of darkness that fell on Egypt long ago. It was so dark we could not see Jesus up on the cross, we could not see each other. We stumbled about in the darkness, enveloped by our grief and sadness at the unspeakable suffering of Jesus. Then out of the darkness we heard a soft barely discernible voice, "My God, my God, why have you forsaken me?" Those of us well versed in scripture immediately recognized it as the opening words of Psalm 22, followed there by the words that Jesus surely wanted us to recall now, "Why are so far from saving me, so far from the words of my groaning? O my God, I cry out by day, but you do not answer, by night, and am not silent. Yet you are enthroned as the Holy One; you are the praise of Israel. In you our fathers put their trust; they trusted and you delivered them." He may not have been able to speak all those words from the psalm in that moment, but he surely wanted us to burn them into our hearts as his life seeped out from him. His invocation of the opening words of Psalm 22 as life was flowing out of him resonated in our spirit for years to come.

Someone from the crowd offered him wine vinegar on a sponge and others shouted out, "Let's see if Elijah comes to save him." Even in this frightful, horrible moment some could not resist jeering at him. How small they seemed. We all turned back to him just as he cried out one last time and then he died right in front of us, hanging on that Roman cross. How truly dark the world seemed in that moment.

Immediately the earth shook beneath our feet and we heard later that the curtain in the holy of holies in the Temple was rent asunder. We could barely stay on our feet, the earth quaking beneath us, rocks tumbling down hills and we learned later that there was even a resurrection of the dead happening in that very moment. We knew the very universe was in upheaval at the death of Jesus. We were not sure at all what to make of it, but it was as if the earth was grieving at Jesus' death. The soldiers were terrified and some of them even proclaimed that Jesus was the son of God. The women present, including Mary Magdelene, Jesus' mother Mary and the mother of the Zebedee boys joined in the grieving and mourning.

We all learned that Joseph of Arimathea, a wealthy business man, approached Pilate and asked for the body of Jesus so he could respectfully and honorably bury him. We were all touched by his gesture. We learned that he prepared the body according to Jewish customs and buried him in a tomb, rolling a stone in front of it. The two Marys sat outside the tomb, comforting each other and sharing their sadness with each other.

I knew I had to get back to Nazareth, to see and talk to Shoshanah and to see how the business was doing. I had been in Jerusalem for several days now but it was time to get home and there was so much to tell Shoshanah. I also needed her advice and counsel to help me figure out exactly what I had seen and learned about during this time with and near Jesus and his apostles. But first there were these frantic reports on Sunday, the third day after the tragic crucifixion, from the apostles that while a contingency of Pharisees and Sadducees had sealed the tomb, now it was empty! We heard that an angel appeared to the Marys and told them that Jesus had, as promised, risen from the dead. The Marys were celebrating and exulting and just then, they reported to the rest of us, Jesus himself appeared to them. They prayed with him and the women told all the apostles that he had instructed the apostles to go back to Galilee where he would appear to them too.

All of us, were, in a word, stunned. This had been the interpretation some had given to the prophecy that he would destroy the Temple and re-build it in three days. Some of the apostles had seen that as a prophecy that he would rise from the dead on the third day after his death, but none of us were sure. We were very familiar with our Jewish teaching about resurrection, that the dead would rise after the messiah had come. But that was always an understanding that all the dead, or at least those whose lives warranted it, would rise. We never had read or studied or learned that one man would rise. This was astounding, first the premise that he had risen from the dead and second, the idea that one who some believed was the messiah had resurrected. Many of us and certainly I among them did not know what to make of this. It was clear that those closest to him believed that the tomb was empty and that he had risen. So many stories and reports and rumors were swirling around Jerusalem on this clear and warm Sunday and it was nearly impossible to make sense of any of it.

The remaining eleven apostles did as they had been told, they returned to Galilee and I along with many other friends and followers went with them. They told us days later that Jesus had indeed come to visit them and instructed them to carry the word of his ministry and teaching to the nations. He let them know that he would always be with them.

I was left with my love for him, my deep affection for everything he had taught us. I heard everything he taught us about loving each other, about loving God and about the coming of the Kingdom of God. I knew that under the threat and the reality of the Roman whip he had acknowledged that he was the messiah, what the Romans called Christ. I knew and in some cases had seen, the wonders and miracles he had performed, including the raising of three people from the dead. I knew all this and still I was left with questions and my own faith crisis. I was home now, with Shoshanah and now I had to plunge deep into my faith and reach my own conclusion about who he was.

Chapter 8

Who Was He?

I am home and I am in turmoil. I just witnessed, was part of, what I am sure are historic moments, events that have the power to change the lives of people here in Israel and perhaps in the far reach of the Roman empire. I was right there, almost in the middle of it all and now I am home and in turmoil. What am I to make of all that happened and how do I answer the ultimate question of it all: Who was he? Who was this Jesus I've known since he was an infant, who I saw grow up like any other child in Nazareth, who I also saw performing impossible acts? I heard him teach, I saw him touch thousands of people, I witnessed for myself how his touch could change people's lives. With all that I am left with the most difficult question of my life: Who was he? Only after I answer that question can I go on to answer what follows: Who am I in relation to him and my faith?

I turned, as I always have in difficult and trying moments, to my beloved wife, Shoshanah. In response to my lifelong inclination to fly high with my wonderings, my imagination, my thoughts of what could be, Shoshanah was always grounded and rational and reasonable. One of the things I love about her is that when I get carried away with some ideas that are new and maybe a bit wild-eyed, Shoshanah calmly talked me through it with serious and critical examination. Shoshanah was my touchstone and I needed her now more than ever.

I started by telling her, sometimes breathlessly I have to admit, all that had happened in Jerusalem. She heard about the parables Jesus taught, the amazing insights he shared with all of us, she heard about the celebratory and then tragic Passover dinner, our last supper with our teacher.

She heard about Jesus' terrible suffering at the hands of the Romans, the taunts and challenges from the Sadduceean priests, the tumult of the crowds, some grieving, some jeering at the sight of Jesus carrying his cross to his crucifixion. I told her about the accounts we had heard of his empty tomb on Sunday, the third day after his execution. She sat raptly while I told her that many had come to believe he was the messiah, especially after being charged by the priests and the Romans and his gentle affirmation of the claim. Those who believed he was the messiah were only strengthened in their faith when they heard about the empty tomb and about his appearances to the Marys and the apostles on two different occasions, in two different places. Many believed the messiah had come and was now dead and three days later, resurrected. They believed that the long-anticipated Jewish messiah had finally come.

"What do you believe, Micah? You were there for almost all of it, you saw what he did, heard what he said. Who was he?" My silence in response disturbed her and it disturbed me even more. She was even more dissatisfied when I finally, in a whisper, said, "I don't know. I don't even know what I believe. I know that I am sad that he died, I know he was not a normal teacher, not just one more sage who came to teach us new ideas. Was he the messiah we have waited and prayed for so long? I don't know."

We sat together silently for a long time. I could hear my heart beating in my chest. Finally I summoned the words to try to make sense of what I could not yet fully grasp or appreciate. "Our sages teach us that the messiah will be a descendant of King David. I always understood that to mean the messiah would do for us what King David had done for the Israelites. David freed our ancestors of all foreign tyrants, foreign subjugation and now his descendant, the messiah, was to do the same for us. This is what the sages taught when they said that when the messiah comes we would see the end of foreign subjugation of Israel. We know that to mean the end of Roman rule."

"And now here we are, a few weeks after Jesus died," Shoshanah interjected, "and Roman rule is as ruthless as ever."

"Yes, we believed all of history would end, all our suffering, our subjugation, our oppression, when the messiah came."

"What do those who believe so strongly say about all that?" Shoshanah asked.

"Some are starting to talk about a second coming, that Jesus came this once to offer us a vision of the Kingdom of God and to offer us God's forgiveness for our sins and that he will return some time in the future. Shoshanah, some are even talking about Jesus himself being God's son."

"We are all God's children, Micah. What does this mean when they talk about Jesus being God's son? Aren't you God's son and I'm God's daughter if we're all God's children?"

I responded hesitantly because this was the part I was having the most trouble understanding. "No, they believe this is different. They believe Jesus is God in the form of the son of the Father. They believe God has three forms, the Father, the Son and the Holy Spirit." Even I was not sure I understood what I was saying, how could Shoshanah?

"But we knew Jesus almost from the time of his birth, from the time he was an infant. He was a normal child, perhaps a bit more gentle than the other children, a bit more serious and less rambunctious, but a child like the others. We saw him grow up and," she stopped herself, "this is wild, the idea that God appears on earth as a human, like a regular person?"

I did not know how to explain this more than what I had already said. "This is what many of the followers are now saying, that Jesus is not only the anticipated messiah, but God Himself appearing among us. There was something about him being fully human, fully divine."

Shoshanah looked at me as seriously and thoughtfully as she ever had and slowly stated, "Micah, nothing has changed since Jesus was here, the world is the same as it always was, Rome is still ruling over Israel ruthlessly. And I know our sages never said anything about God being able to appear in physical, human form. That, quite simply, contradicts everything scripture and our sages say about God."

I could certainly not disagree with what Shoshanah was saying and as usual she spoke directly to my heart. "I know what you are saying. In Deuteronomy (6:5) we declare and we say it twice every day, 'Hear O Israel, the Lord is our God, the Lord is one." One, not three, I knew that was the central statement of our faith about God. "But some of the followers are pointing to other places in scripture, like in the creation story where God speaks about Himself in the plural and they talk about places like in Exodus where Moses sees God in physical form. It is all so confounding and confusing."

Shoshanah, love of my life, the wife of my youth, made it very clear she could not, did not believe Jesus was messiah and she certainly did not believe he was any more the child of God than any of the rest of us. She also made it clear that she recognized that I had had these experiences with him and that she understood I would have to make my own decision about my faith.

I did what I had always done in moments of emotional and spiritual turmoil, I walked. The hills surrounding Nazareth were the places of my spiritual refuge and so I walked. For what seemed like hours, I walked the familiar hills, long my refuge in difficult moments. No moment before in my life was like this one. I admired Jesus as a young man, I had grown to love his teachings, his message of faith and love and inclusion. I knew that I had learned from him how to make sure the weakest and most marginalized among us were included in our circle of love and compassion. I knew that I had learned from him how to love everyone, especially the weak, the impaired, the vulnerable as God loved each one of us. He had taught me and so many others how to live our lives more in line with what God wanted of us. He focused less on the commandments and obligations of our traditional teachings and more about love. He never suggested we abandon Shabbat rituals or the obligations of other holidays and festivals or the tenets of the dietary restrictions of scripture but he did tell us to pay closer attention to priorities and to make the spiritual content of our actions be more important than the physical fulfillment of commandments. He was the one who taught me that God wanted us to go beyond the physical fulfillment of the commandment and look at the spiritual content even more.

But was he the messiah and even more difficult, was he God's son living among us? We had never learned this idea that the messiah would be God Himself in human form. We knew the messiah was the one God would anoint to bring about an end to our suffering and oppression. Shoshanah was right, the suffering and subjugation had not ended and was, if anything, worse than ever. Were we supposed to wait for a second coming and would that come in weeks or months or years? Some of his followers insisted we did not understand his teachings if we thought the physical world would change with his coming, what they called the first coming. They insisted that what had changed was not the end of foreign subjugation but our own spiritual subjugation. He rose from the dead, they insisted, to demonstrate to the non-believers that he was now with God, the Father. They proclaimed that everything that mattered changed—our spirits, our relationship to God, our faith and our ultimate destiny to live with God in heaven. The apostles especially told us that if we focused on the physical, the rule of Rome or any other empire, we were missing Jesus' teaching from as early as what we were starting to call the Sermon on the Mount on the shores of the Sea of Galilee. Peter himself said that if we looked only to whether Rome was still ruling Israel or the other physical appearance of history then we had never really listened to Jesus.

So, I was left with my question that I knew I had to answer—who was he? Who was this child of Nazareth, grown into a remarkable man, scorned by many and serene to the very end? I was there with him through so much of it, from his youth, his time as a child spending time in my own home with our daughter, Rachel to his death on the cross. I was there, I had to know who he was, whether the stories of the resurrection were true or only wishful thinking and rumors.

After hours of solitude and my own personal spiritual journey I came to know what was true for me, what my faith declared. Jesus was a man, a great sage, a man I admired so greatly, from whom I had learned so much. No matter how great he was, I believe that he was not the messiah we had waited for and not God in human form. I believed the teachings of our sages about the messiah and the impossibility of God appearing in human form. If God was also human, then God had to be tall or short, skinny or fat, one color skin or another, male or female and I could not accept those limitations for God. I did not believe, as some of the apostles were teaching, that the prophets, especially Isaiah, had anticipated the coming of Jesus. I knew that our teachings had always held that the prophets' messages were for their own times, not for a distant future of hundreds or even thousands of years. I could not accept their interpretation of key passages to be foreshadowing of the coming of Jesus into our lives.

I knew that no matter how sure I was in my faith regarding Jesus, that the apostles would be disappointed in me. I knew that they believed I was being blind to the true character of Jesus. I also knew what I believe as a Jew living in these tumultuous times. My faith and the teachings of my sages told me that what ultimately mattered was our fulfillment of God's commandments regardless of the spirit that went with them. I did not believe that lust was essentially the same as committing adultery as Jesus had taught in the Sermon on the Mount and that it was simply impossible to go through life without being angry. God expected me not to kill, not to have sexual relations with another man's wife, not to take an oath lightly, and I accepted the Torah's teaching on divorce. I loved much of what Jesus taught but there were elements that conflicted with what I understood from Torah and our sages and I could not accept some of what he had said.

Was it possible to admire, respect, even love Jesus and not believe he was the messiah and son of God? Could I, a Jew, consider myself a follower, even a student of Jesus and not accept the conclusion of the apostles and many of his students? It was becoming increasingly clear that our Jewish people were divided and in some cases, even hostile to each other on these questions. When I spoke to those who did believe he was the Jewish messiah and told them of my faith some became angry and made ugly accusations. They told me I was blind, that I could not see what had been right in front of me. We were all Jews, but over the months and years after his death it was as if we were becoming like the Pharisees and Sadducees, fierce opponents of each other. I hated the acrimony within our community and I could not, at the same time, see a resolution. Some were fully committed to the belief that Jesus was the messiah we had waited for and came to believe he would come again. Others of us looked around us and were just as filled with faith that he was not the promised messiah. Many of course just continued with their work and their families and did not take a position one way or the other. But for those of us who had been touched by his faith, by his teachings and his actions we were moving into one camp of faith or another.

One of his most devoted followers, a fellow Jew from Nazareth, someone I had known for years, confronted me one day. Because he approached me with less anger than most did I was willing to have the conversation with him. Baruch had always been level headed and had also been with Jesus since very near the beginning and he believed he was the messiah and son of God.

"Micah," Baruch started, "you saw him raise the dead back to life, in fact three times he did it and each time the person had been dead longer than the one before. How can that not convince you he was or is the messiah and son of God?"

"Baruch, you know scripture as well as I do. The prophet Elijah and his student and successor, Elisha, also raised the dead back to life and in fact, they also did it three times and you will recall that with the three they resurrected, they were also increasingly dead." I knew it was an awkward way to phrase it, but Baruch knew that I meant that the three people Elijah and Elisha raised from the dead had been, in successive order, dead longer than the ones before them. "Baruch, you are surely aware of the parallels in the case of our prophets of old and now Jesus. They were not the messiah and I do not believe Jesus is either. They were careful to give credit to God and it was a reflection of their intimate relationship with God that they could bring the dead back to life. That cannot be the proof or evidence that Jesus is the messiah."

"Oh, Micah, you refuse to see what is right in front of you. How about the times we saw him, with our own eyes, heal the sick, the lame, the ones possessed by Satan? Surely those miracles prove Jesus is the messiah, son of God."

"Baruch," I responded just as firmly and resolutely, "you know the stories of Honi the Circle Drawer, how he went from community to community and prayed for it to rain and it would rain. You know how that one time he could not get the rain to fall from the skies he drew a circle in the earth and proclaimed he would not move from the circle until rain fell to the ground. What a moment it was when it started to rain. Baruch, you know that if a person performs a miracle that does not mean he is the messiah we have waited for. You know that God will work with certain people of pious devotion and faith to perform miracles. The fact is that history, our people's story and experience here in Israel, has not changed at all since Jesus was here and died. Baruch, I cannot and do not believe Jesus is the messiah, no matter how much I admire, even love him."

I knew that I could never convince Baruch and he was not going to convince me. I had the same conversations with Peter and some of the other apostles and we ended up having to agree that we could not reach the same conclusion about Jesus. We Jews were united on so many things, on so many matters of faith and practice and on this so many of us were in disagreement and divided. We all loved God and had faith that he would some day save Israel and we all certainly agreed that that was the origin of Jesus' name, like Joshua in scripture. We could simply not agree on who he was and is and that was cause for considerable sadness. I knew that my relationship with Peter and the other apostles was now strained, we still loved each other but we were now following different paths. I had to accept that we would all continue to be Jews, faithful to God and our people, but that we now had to disagree on whether Jesus of Nazareth was the anointed one of God.

Stories and reports were beginning to circulate, long after I could travel from my home in Nazareth, about a new follower, a bold and adventurous Jew named Saul from Tarsus. His family, we heard, had moved from Tarsus which is north of Syria, to Jerusalem and it seems he grew up there, a few years younger than Jesus and my own Rachel. It seems he became, as a young adult, quite the critic of Jesus and his followers. After Jesus' death he even worked with the priests and elders to prosecute and persecute some of the faithful followers of Jesus. I never met him but there were these strange and intriguing stories about this young man. Apparently it was on a journey to Damascus where he was intent on apprehending

Jewish followers of Jesus and bring them back to Jerusalem that he had some kind of revelation experience and saw the risen Jesus. We learned that Saul became Paul and he transformed into one of Jesus' most energetic and avid followers. He argued with the followers in Jerusalem about issues like whether non-Jews who wanted to follow Jesus had to follow the Jewish laws of kashrut and circumcision. He insisted that now that the messiah had come people who believed in him did not have to adhere to Jewish law. It was apparently quite the argument with the Jerusalem faithful and Paul seemed to win the day.

Paul became the peripatetic follower, traveling throughout the empire, from Asia Minor to Rome itself to talk to anyone who would listen about his faith in Jesus and the ways in which faith in Jesus could bring about their salvation. There was no town or public place too far, too remote for him to come and talk to the people and witness to his faith and draw them in. Pagans by the thousands became devoted to Jesus and the kingdom of God he had brought to all the people. Increasingly there was this dilemma about whether these people were now Jews since they did not follow Jewish law and did not convert to Judaism. More and more there was this divide between the Jews like me who did not believe Jesus was the messiah or son of God and those Jews who did believe and the pagans who now believed he was the Jewish messiah. I could only anticipate that future generations of our people, here in Israel and throughout the Roman empire were going to be driven further apart by these divisions. I could only wonder and imagine how all this would be resolved for my children and grandchildren. I sensed that these questions of faith and identity were only going to pull our people apart in ways that we could not fully understand just fifteen years after the death of Jesus.

I knew that I was approaching the end of my life. It had been some amazing journey, with my beloved Shoshanah, our daughter Rachel and the boys, Shlomo and Gavriel. Shoshanah had always been my rock, my sounding board, the voice of measured analysis and critical thinking when I got carried away with the emotion of the moment. She was the one I could tell anything and everything about what I was witnessing and experiencing and she was the one who would gently bring me back to reality and quiet thought.

The children were the pride of my life and our first-born, Rachel, had been a close friend of Jesus in their childhood but rarely saw or talked to him once he left Nazareth for Capernaum, the other towns of the Galilee and Jerusalem. As a young woman she married and gave birth to my first grandchild, Avi. As my life energy slowly seeped from my body, I looked at the baby Avi and wondered what his life and faith would look like.

He was my future and also the future of the Jewish people during these tumultuous times. I had to wonder what his life and faith would look like in decades to come.

Post-Script

Two Generations Later

My name is Avi, son of Chayim, grandson of Micah. Like my father and the fathers before him, I live in Nazareth, in the Galilee and I tend olive trees for the olives and the precious oil. My wife, Sarah, and I get by with our five children during times that have been difficult for as long as anyone in my family can remember. Recently I found the document my grandfather Micah wrote years ago in a pottery jar none of us had noticed before. The jar broke when the children were playing and out tumbled the pages Micah had written. I am told that my grandfather was a great man, a man who had known Jesus of Nazareth from the time the baby was brought to Nazareth by Mary and Joseph. When I was a child my grandfather told me his stories, about his being a young man when Jesus was brought to Nazareth by his parents and how he got to watch the boy grow up. I learned so much from him about what he saw Jesus do and teach and about my grandfather's admiration and love for Jesus. He also told me about the horribly painful suffering and death of Jesus and the debates he and his friends had about who Jesus was. He told me about his conclusion that Jesus was not the messiah, son of God and how that created some debate and division between him and the ardent apostles and followers.

I was there, just outside his room, when my grandfather, Micah died. As he had been during his life, so he was when he died, quiet and gentle, his strength slowly ebbing out of his life. I was sad, my mother Rachel, his daughter was really sad, but I knew he had lived a good and long life, had seen and experienced so much and was such a good man. Before the moment came he had told us all his time had come and he was ready to go to Olam Haba (the world to come). As always, he was dignified and composed.

After he died, after the period of shiva (seven days of mourning) were over and we all returned to our normal activities I read Micah's document that he had stored away in the jar. I had told him about finding it and he asked me to read it after he died. He urged me to write my own reactions and then store it all away again so perhaps future generations could read what we had written together. I read every word of what he wrote and while there were not big surprises because I had heard so many stories while sitting with him those last years, I was touched by his love and faith. For reasons I can only vaguely recall now, decades later, I did not honor his request that I write about my reactions to what I had learned from him. Maybe it was too early, maybe more years had to pass for me to share what I understood about Jesus of Nazareth and the movement that began during his life and which continued long after his death. It is now some forty years after my beloved grandfather Micah's death, sixty years after the crucifixion of Jesus and I, Micah's grandson, am now facing the end of my own journey. I have seen so much myself and now it is time for me to share what I have seen, to share my own faith all these years later.

Ah, what I have seen during these years. Micah wrote about his experiences with Jesus and I know he admired, even loved the boy and the man. He was witness to so much that happened during the nearly three years of Jesus' ministry in Galilee and Jerusalem. I also know that he had to reach his own conclusion about Jesus and who he believed Jesus was. Micah's faith drew him to conclude that Jesus was not the messiah or son of God that he and his apostles claimed. None of that diminished Micah's admiration of and love for Jesus. He wrote about Saul of Tarsus, who became Paul, the greatest messenger of faith in Jesus. Paul traveled the world we know to share his faith, to share the words and life of Jesus and he persuaded thousands of people to come to believe in Jesus. Paul and the other apostles drew people to the Jewish messiah so that it became a movement of faith throughout the Roman empire.

The most difficult years of my life came when our people rebelled against Rome in a heroic uprising that was doomed from the start but which grew out of our surging rage over Roman rule. It was around the same time we heard about the death of Paul in Rome. Florus, the Roman procurator in Jerusalem, stole silver from the holy Temple in Jerusalem. This was merely the latest and last Roman outrage against our people and the sanctity of the Temple. Nero was emperor in Rome and his rule was as oppressive and tyrannical as any who came before him. We all knew a rebellion against Rome could not succeed, especially once they sent soldiers in from their encampments in Syria. We may have been doomed from the start but our dignity and our faith demanded we act.

Not all of our people supported the rebellion and this was one more reason we could not succeed. Some believed we were only dooming ourselves to massacre at the hands of Roman soldiers and some of the most outspoken opponents of our rebellion were the followers of Jesus. These were fellow Jews who insisted our rebellion was misguided, even corrupt. They believed, nearly forty years after the death of Jesus, that the kingdom of God was imminent and that our rebellion was an expression of our lack of faith. As events unfolded it became increasingly clear that those of us who supported the rebellion had to fight the Romans and our fellow Jews who opposed the fight at the same time. With the divisions inside our own community and the fierce military actions of the Roman army it became clear we would fail and many would die.

In the summer of the fifth year of the rebellion Rome had defeated our rebel fighters throughout Israel and now were set on retaking Jerusalem and the Temple itself. Those who were there on those hot days of summer reported to the rest of us how the soldiers attacked the city and captured the holy Temple which had stood, in various forms, for nearly a thousand years, since the time of our King Solomon. We made offerings to God there and only there, acts which drew us closer to God. We had begun to offer prayers in our local synagogues in recent years, but our primary way to draw close to God was through the commanded offerings at the Temple. We learned about the Roman conquest of the Temple and the flames that rose up from the magnificent structure. Our people had no way to make these sacred offerings and the very center of our faith and tradition was destroyed. The rebellion had failed and it appeared we were doomed.

I did hear stories a few years later about a small community of zealous Jews who held out against the Romans at Masada, a mountain fortress on the shore of the Salt (or, Dead) Sea. These intrepid zealots apparently had food and weapons to last them years and they held out against the Roman forces for three years. I was grieved again to learn of the Roman success in defeating the Masada encampment. Apparently they reached the top of the flat-top mountain only to find the Jews had all killed themselves in an act of Kiddush Hashem (martyrdom in the name of God). They chose to die by each other's hands rather than give the Romans the pleasure of killing the men and enslaving the women and children. Apparently a few women and children hid out and later escaped to tell us all their tale of resistance.

In the immediate years after the revolt the divisions and animosity with our Jewish community were intense. Those of us who supported the revolt believed that those who opposed us, including the followers of Jesus had doomed our valiant efforts. The Jesus faithful believed the revolt was misguided and a failure of faith. We were so angry with each other and the divide between those who believed in Jesus and those who did not only grew. There had been some division between us as a result of Paul's decree that people could become followers of the Jewish messiah without adhering to Jewish law. Many of us argued that a person could not be a Jew without keeping kosher and observing Shabbat and we reminded Paul and his supporters that even Jesus himself said he had not come to abolish the law. We saw this as a total break from Jewish tradition and practice and that this position of his put his pagan followers outside the Jewish community. There was no resolution to the matter but there was this tension between us, a division between the Jews who believed in Jesus and those who did not.

Now it was some twenty years after the great revolt in Jerusalem, over twenty years since the death of Paul and we had no rebellions left and our internal disagreements had only grown. There was only a small community of Jews left in Jerusalem, most of our people lived in Galilee, along the Mediterranean coast, in Syria and other parts of the Roman empire. There was a growing Jewish community in the east, in Babylonia and they were establishing their own academies of study.

All of us, here in Israel and in Babylonia, had a difficult task—how would we serve God, draw close to God, without our offerings at the Temple in Jerusalem. There were no longer any priests, no Sadducees without the Temple, no way to make offerings. During these last twenty years since the cataclysm of the Destruction our sages began using the title, Rabbi, or teacher. Their task was to study the writings and traditions of our people and create ways to apply them to our daily lives. One of the developments they were working on was a body of liturgy, prayers that we would offer three times a day, on Shabbat and other holidays and for occasions and moments during the day. We began gathering together in synagogues around the Roman empire to study together and offer prayers that drew us closer to God. We began to understand that these prayers would substitute for the Temple offerings and the rabbis used the model of the offering schedule to create the structure of our prayers.

We also had to reach some conclusion about the divide between us about the faith in Jesus that some among us had. I continued in the faith of my parents and grandparents, that Jesus was a good and devoted man who taught great ideas and taught us powerful lessons but that he was not the messiah or son of God. The division between those of us who did not believe Jesus was the anticipated Jewish messiah, the anointed one of God and those who did had grown too great to be able to think of us as one community. It was increasingly clear to all of us that the believers in Jesus, now including great numbers of pagans drawn to the faith by Paul, were part of a separate and distinct faith community. Some were even calling them by the name, Christians, derived from the Greek word for messiah, Christ. They were now calling the one they believed to be the messiah, Jesus Christ.

As I approached the end of my life I could tell that we were going to be Jews and Christians, no longer all Jews divided by the question of our faith about Jesus. Due to the missionary efforts of the students of Paul and the apostles, the numbers of these new Christians were growing substantially. My grandfather, Micah, never could have imagined we would reach this point, a separation between us based on our faith. He could never have imagined there would be Jews and Christians, but the best I can tell, this is how it is going to be for our people.

While I see increasing tension between our faith communities I pray that we can always remember that we are all children of God, descendants, at least spiritually, of Abraham and Moses. I fear the future but I have great hope as well. I will pray until my final moment that we can live together in love and faith, remembering that what unites us, our faith in God, is so much greater than what divides us. In my final days I offer this one prayer, "Bayom ha-hu yihyeh Adonai echad ushmo echad." "On that day there will be one God and his name shall be one."

67185550R00115

Made in the USA
Charleston, SC
06 February 2017